These Are Not Sweet Girls

These Are Not Sweet Girls

Latin American Women Poets

Edited by
Marjorie Agosín

WHITE PINE PRESS · BUFFALO, NEW YORK

Acknowledgments:
I wish to thank Wellesley College for granting me a sabbatical
that allowed me the time to compile this anthology.

"Speaking of Gabriel," "The Parable of the Unfaithful Wife," "Silence Around an
Ancient Stone," "The Return," "Meditation on the Threshold," "Poetry is Not You,"
"Origin," "Destiny," and "The Farewell" copyright 1988 by the Estate of Rosario
Castellanos. Translation copyright 1988 by Magda Bogin. Reprinted from *The
Selected Poems of Rosario Castellanos* with the permission of Graywolf Press, Saint
Paul, Minnesota.

"Murmur," "Heart's Desire," "Serenade," "Successive Deaths," and "Easter" copy-
right 1990 by Adelia Prado. Translation copyright 1990 by Ellen Watson. Reprinted
from *The Alphabet in the Park*, Wesleyan University Press, with the permission of
University Press of New England.

"A letter comes and visits me," "Letters are not letters because they dream," "Ask,"
"I have been a fortune teller," and "I am the shepherd of hope" copyright 1994 by
Giannina Braschi. Translations copyright 1994 by Tess O'Dwyer. Reprinted from
Empire of Dreams with the permission of Yale University Press.

Acknowledgments continue on page 367.

Publication of this book was made possible, in part, by a grant from the
Chrysopolae Foundation, the National Endowment for the Arts, and with
public funds from the New York State Council on the Arts, a state agency.

Book design: Elaine LaMattina

Cover: Woodcut, 18" x 24", "Mirror's Dream," by Emma Alvarez Piñeiro.

Manufactured in the United States of America.

9 8 7 6 5 4 3 2

Published by White Pine Press, P.O. Box 236, Buffalo, NY 14201

EDITOR'S ACKNOWLEDGEMENTS

Words, their incantatory shapes and melodies, their power and lucidity, are part of my childhood and my future. I grew up with poets and their words. I belong to a country that continues to be proud of its poetic legacy, and I have inherited its alphabet and sounds. Before I learned to read, my mother, aunts, and nannies recited poetry to me. This anthology belongs to them and to the wisdom of their teachings.

During my years at Wellesley College my students and I have shared the gift of poetry both outside and inside the classroom. Poetry has taught and enchanted us. We learned to repect her ways and above all to appreciate poetry's way of being part of our memories. This anthology is the gift of students and teachers united by the threads of poetry and its textures. I want especially to thank Monica Bruno, Monica Molina, and Claudia Muñoz for working with me in many ways on this project.

Translators deserve special thanks for their dedication and their generosity. They have taught me that you can cross the imaginary borders of language. Special thanks to Emma Sepúlveda-Pulvirenti and Shawn T. Griffin for their inspiration. Also to Celeste Kostopulos-Cooperman for her eloquent Afterword, for reading the manuscript, and for good coffee and conversation about poetry and children.

Throughout the years I have been nurtured and inspired by my editors at White Pine Press, Dennis Maloney and Elaine LaMattina. Special thanks to Elaine, who has laboriously worked on this manuscript with generosity and infinite patience. Without her, this anthology would not have been possible.

The love of my husband, my children, my friend Allison Khalil, her two children, and her husband, the constant conversations of my parents about poetry and language, about the value of translation, has nourished me during the completion of *These Are Not Sweet Girls*. I am grateful for their enduring love and their belief in my true vocation: poetry.

The poets in this anthology are true protagonists of this text. They have sung songs of sorrow, shadows, exile and return. I thank them for their strength and for leading us on this magnificent journey through women's words.

To the valiant women poets of Latin America
who dared to speak
·

To my daughter Sonia Helena
who is beginning to speak

CONTENTS

· ·

THESE ARE NOT THE SWEET GIRLS

CLOSE TO ME

SILENCE THAT CAN BE HEARD

THE MOON'S CADAVER

GESTURES FROM MY WINDOW

TO BE SEVENTEEN AGAIN

These Are Not Sweet Girls

INTRODUCTION

"Poets who compile anthologies should be scrupulously honest in including only poems they genuinely admire. Anthologies are poetry's gateway to the general culture. They should not be used as pork barrels for the creative writing trade. An art expands itself by producing masterpieces not mediocrity. Anthologies should be compiled to move, delight, and instruct readers not to flatten the writing teachers who assign books."

— Dana Gioia
The Atlantic Monthly, May 1991

Throughout history, women have been closer to words than to silence. Talking, singing and whispering continue to be the means through which women learn and through which they practice the art of communicating. They comunicate not only through the written word but through a variety of media. In Chile, women record stories in multi-colored tapestries called *arpilleras,* where fragments and elements of everyday life become paintings created with scraps, offerings to life and death. There, the feminine text opens up like a linen of plentitude and possibility. Women write to record their history and as part of a common legacy which identifies them with their culture.

Though women have always been close to words, they have often been barred from speaking: Saint Paul, in the Holy Scriptures, ordered women to be silent in church, thus censuring their means of public expression. Numerous cultural maxims that attempt to predispose women to remain silent have been internalized by the female psyche, e.g., "En boca cerrada no entran moscas." ("No flies will enter a closed mouth.") Yet women have continued speaking their minds, often through the sacred language of poetry, where there is an abundance of intuition and the possibility of reclaiming power through language.

Latin American poetry, an interesting phenomenon in its own right, is different from Anglo-Saxon poetry, as well as that of other regions in the West. In Latin America, creating poetry is a common skill, one that is deeply rooted in people's everyday lives. Cleaning ladies, priests and academics all recite the same verses remembered from childhood. They all attend the same poetry readings, which sometimes are more popular than sports events, another unusual characteristic of Latin American poetry. Given the universality of poetry within these societies, it is easy to understand how it is applied to all facets of life and is used in slogans as well as in children's lullabies.

Those devoted to the study of Latin American poetry can identify the names of poets such as Vicente Huidobro, Pablo Neruda, and César Vallejo, all twentieth century male poets. It is only because she won the Nobel Prize for Literature in 1945 that Gabriela Mistral's voice is not ignored. Male critics have often ascribed the poetry of women such as Mistral to the ideology that they represent; at other times, they have simply denied or ignored the literary production of women. The poetry of these women, created in patriarchal societies, has not achieved recognition within the canon of contemporary literature. In general, anthologies of Latin American poetry include very few women. *The Penguin Handbook of Latin American Verse* includes four women and seventy-six men.

After the 1970s, with the proliferation of research regarding women's issues, new editions and sporadic reprints of women's texts began to appear. In the United States, two new anthologies began to fill the vacuum in the field of Latin American women's poetry: *Open to the Sun* (1987) and *Women Who Have Sprouted Wings* (1989). To date, *Ixok Amar Go* (1992) is the only anthology about Central American women poets.

This anthology is an alternative type of text. It is not all-encompassing, nor does it pretend to catalogue the authors according to a geographical space. I chose texts from voices that come from within, voices that speak and view the world from a woman's perspective. The poems presented here point toward a specific gender and identify themselves with the author's condition as a woman.

These poems also subvert the order of traditional anthologies. For example, placing the ever-popular folk voice of someone like Violeta Parra together with the more recent, bolder poetry of Alejandra Pizarnik does not fit the traditional scheme. Some of the poets, for example Puerto Rican poet Olga Nolla and Costa Rican Ana Istarú, are represented with a significant body of work. Others, such as Mexico's Pita Amor and Peru's Laura Riesco, are represented by a brief selection. The criteria for choosing the amount of poetry speaks once again about the ideology and criteria of this anthology: to present the finest poems I have come across.

I have been approaching the texts of Latin American women writers and preparing this anthology for approximately three years. I collected an array of images, and I identified with them, with the vision of a poet who sees herself in the words of others. One of the most revealing facets of my research was that one can gather the voices of various generations of poets and join them to form a unified landscape. For example, we have Delmira Agustini, the first erotic poet from Uruguay, next to Ana Istarú, a contemporary Costa Rican voice whose poetry does not mimic that of the older generation but nevertheless implies a common tradition and contains similar metaphors.

While gathering these poems, I decided to include authors whose work has never appeared in any anthology of Latin American literature and who have not been part of an official canon, such as Honduran poet Clementina Suárez, unknown outside her country, yet one of the most prominent figures of Central America. I also included two Bolivian poets, Blanca Wiethüchter and Yolanda Bedregal, whose works, to date, had been unpublished in English. I have attempted to maintain the balance, as well as the union, between well-known figures such as Rosario Castellanos and Alfonsina Storni and not so well-known writers such as Elsa Cross and Perla Schwartz, both from Mexico, or Jeannette Miller from the Dominican Republic.

The reader will be surprised by the variety of texts, voices and textures. It is almost as if the women themselves had been gathered here, forming a mosaic of voices filled with the enormous power of language and individuality. In each one of these women there exists an obsession with speaking and writing, with subverting traditions. The Chilean Cecilia Vicuña is a major example of this phenomenon: in the majority of her texts, the thought of creating words is intertwined with the act of loving. I have observed through these diverse yet similar voices that women's poetry is not charged with sentimentality and baroque elements. In most cases, their poetry is introspective, deep, and preoccupied with the intricacies of language with the meaning of being and language. Unlike the autobiographical and confessional texts that have characterized Latin American women since colonial times, these poems go beyond a tradition of writing as a duty or as penance. The poets in this anthology defy and transcend the common stereotype of the submissive and abnegated woman. Instead, what we see is a group of women creating powerful images, women who defy us with their every word.

These texts are also united by a tangible pleasure derived from the taste of words, from the poets' breath and from their bodies. The poets are not the characters of their texts; they are the narrators of their own destinies. The body of the poem, like the human body, appears in these texts as a way of confronting archaic language and assessing these women's sense of familiarity and ease with their bodies and with open language.

Although it is difficult to speak of a women's poetic tradition and to define them as modernists or post-modernists, minimalists or Baroques, I believe that these texts demonstrate that there is a women poets' "culture" that recreates history in an isolated, yet collective, way. As poetry readings gained new significance in the Southern Cone — where there has been a perverse and silent conspiracy surrounding women's literature, especially during the years of the dictatorships — a new way to approach the texts of women was suggested. Women reflected upon their work and attempted, through their writings, to redefine literary alliances and build on the direct communication that existed between the various generations of writers.

Editors have often separated the voices of Southern and Central American writers in an attempt to distance them and detach them from a common history. This anthology should be read as a journey upon which the authors intend to shape a literary and historical tradition of their own. The poets represent many areas of Latin America, such as Argentina, Cuba, Bolivia, the Dominican Republic, Uruguay, and Chile. Bonds are created between the texts of these poets, establishing the creation of a women's poetic tradition.

The object of this anthology, then, is to unmask the official discourse of power that has kept women's poetic speech outside of the literary mainstream. This anthology coincides with a pluralistic and decentralized discourse: although love, sex, and desire appear in most of the poems, they are not repressed or silenced emotions but rather tools in these women's search for pleasure through the use of words and the body.

The most notable characteristic of the poets presented in this anthology resides in their courage and inventiveness. These poets, especially those born at the turn of the century, are bold in their writing; their poetry is daring and, therefore, different from that written by their male contemporaries. One such poet is Clementina Suárez, whose texts give the impression of being contemporary:

> *I have watched myself being born,*
> *grow without a sound,*
> *without branches that hurt like arms*
> *Subtle, silent, without words to hurt .*
> *. .*

and

> *I stepped out of my dress*
> *and I stumbled upon my body*
> *then I could understand*
> *the value of my feet, my hands and*
> *my legs*
> *my stomach and my sex, my eyes*
> *and my face.*

Suárez's voice proclaims an encounter with the body, and it is this metaphor of the nude that will become one of the unifying elements in the poetry of these women. When I began the difficult task of organizing and grouping these texts, I suddenly realized how they flowed; I saw their similarities, the common metaphors, and the openly sensual and revealing imagery. I observed that these women's poems were not grandiloquent or heroic, but rather, personal and historical as well. The criteria used to group them into sections were mostly thematic. That way, I wove the sections together like bright tapestries of women's voices.

"Like the Magic Glow of a Paradise" begins this anthology, containing poems linked by love, desire, and writing. Clementina Suárez, Delmira Agustini, Idea Vilariño, Ana Istarú, Cristina Peri Rossi, and Julia de Burgos form an extraordinary alliance in search of language, in search of a common voice and identity. Cristina Peri Rossi frames her creation with images of voyagers in order to speak about the submerged body and about love's secrets:

> *Cover her with herbs and plants.*
> *Bring from far away tiny leaves*
> *filaments of stalks*
> *fresh flowers.*

Through these images, Peri Rossi invokes the female body and desire. In Ana Istarú's poetry, we see the male body depicted in all its splendor, but it is the female body that seeks and provides love and nourishment:

> *Where have you come from*
> *sleeping man*
> *what cloud spilled you,*
> *what caravel?*

Puerto Rican poet Julia de Burgos and Uruguayan Delmira Agustini are united in an unexpected way, de Burgos searching for desire and love and Agustini searching for freedom to love. Linked for the first time when speaking from the perspective of and about the history of love and absence, recreating the adventures of those lost, either on an abandoned island or an abandoned body, placing the poetry of these two women in the same section is the starting point for revising and altering the traditional canon of women's poetry. Also included in this first section is the vibrant work of Cuba's most venerated poet Dulce María Loynaz. Winner of the Cervantes Prize for Literature, her work is practically unknown in English. And like Suárez, Loynaz's work, since the early 1920s is filled with a sense of unabashed freedom and eroticism. Carlota Caulfield, a Cuban-Irish poet who now lives in California, shares with her contemporaries like Ana Istarú and Cristina Peri Rossi a powerful mixture of antiquity and modernity – a poetry filled with images of mythical times and their places skillfully woven into a language filled with the resonance of a voyage of self-discovery. Caulfield portrays in this selection the unmasked figure of a traveler who discovers the power of her inner journey, which is the journey toward herself and "the threads of her own passion

In "These Are Not the Sweet Girls," the second section of this anthology, we see the surprising similarities between the renowned Mexican poet Rosario Castellanos and the young Peruvian poet Giovanna Pollarolo. The lyrical voices in this section subvert and rebel against routine; they speak about it as if it were a prison. The poets rebel through language which casts a light on and makes of their everyday lives a battlefield where objects become the signifiers of disorder and of liberty. Olga Nolla, from Puerto Rico, is one of the most original and daring voices of the Caribbean. Her poetry is marked by irreverence to the status quo, to bourgeois society and to man's domination of society. Her poem "Manifesto" exemplifies this vibrant new generation of writers. In this section, as well as in the section dedicated to love and desire, we observe a clearly defined path from the legendary sayings to the poems of Rosario Castellanos, who proposes "another way of being," to the elegant and ironical poems of Giovanna Pollarolo who says: "What would we talk about before, I ask, when we had neither children nor husbands, nor maids?" Paz Molina is one of Chile's most original and provocative poets of her generation. A contemporary of Olga Nolla, her irony and contempt for male/female relationshilps, her spirit of defiance, make her heir to Rosario Castellanos' poetics. In her work the complexities of love and its misfortunes come alive: "I am innocent of the storm / the gods have sworn to protect me."

The section titled "Close to Me" gathers voices that, at first glance, appear different in tone and in origin. Magali Alabau is a Cuban poet living in New York; Alaide Foppa was a human rights activist from Guatemala who disappeared in the late 1960s. What is extraordinary is that in this section the mosaic of voices reflect the experiences of brotherhood and sisterhood. Alfonsina Storni, considered to be a subversive, a radical for Argentina's bourgeois, appears next to Chilean Gabriela Mistral who has been canonized as the Saint Mother, yet we see that Storni's poems both in image and meaning are more traditional than Mistral's: Mistral was an advocate for human rights and the plight of the Indian long before those concerns became fashionable. Aida Cartagena de Portalatin, the Dominican Republic's most distinguished poet, is often catalogued as an avant garde artist, yet in these poems she reveals her profound adherence to what often has been called a socialist motherhood. Also in this section is the poetry of Cuba's Nancy Morejon, one of the island's most distinguished poets and known for her ardent support of the Cuban Revolution; yet in this gathering of poems, the reader will find a lyricism in Morejon's work different from her early political poetry. Poems of motherhood to nostalgic evocations of Havana speak of lost and yet renewed landscapes of an island mythicized by its own dreams. The official image of Gabriela Mistral violates all cultural stereotypes since her poems to mothers, women and children are filled with a deep ideological content that goes beyond that of a teacher preoccupied with the future of her pupils. In the poems by Mistral included in this anthology, we get a glimpse of her powerful imagination and figurative language based on minute elements. Her poetry is often stripped of the traditional metaphors associated with the poetic language employed by the women of her time. Mistral's voice, depicted in melodious lullabies and fantastic stories, appears next to Alaide Foppa's, who found in herself the voices of her children and the pain of the women who had lost their children. Foppa and Mistral, therefore, share a bond through maternity and the discovery of the body. In the lyrical poems of the Puerto Rican poet María Arrillaga, the traditional vision of motherhood becomes a powerful way of revealing how the threads of women's familiar conversations bind together women who have been empowered by their alliances as sisters, poets, and visionaries. Arrillaga uses the image of the "female guerrilla" to create the emblematic figure of a new female validated by her wisdom and her language.

"Silence that Can be Heard" is an integral part of this anthology. Beginning in the 1970s, women have had a powerful role in the development of human rights. Many of them began their artistic careers in the line of fire and used their pen and paper to reveal the truth and to extirpate the horror created by the fearsome tyrannies of Latin America. In this section, we have texts by women poets who remember their disappeared friends and annihilated generation. Amanda Berenguer speaks about horrible tortures. Gioconda Belli loves and fights in a Nicaragua that is free yet captive at the same time. Emma Sepúlveda-Pulvirenti recreates dates and anniversaries of deaths and departures. All of these authors are linked through the concept that poetry is, in itself, an instrument of power, of change and of liberation. As I was completing this anthology, I received a call from Meredith Tax, president of PEN's Women's Committee. She was excited about the work of Belinda Zubicueta Carmona. A Chilean poet born in the same year I was born, her destiny led her to the somber chambers of state terror. Belinda was the longest-held political prisoner during the Pinochet dictatorship. While in prison, she wrote poetry that spoke of censorship and fear but also of the hope beyond the prison walls and of poetry's victorious sound. Belinda remained a prisoner during the coming of democracy in Chile, and she was only recently released. Both her poetry and her life speak of strength under adversity. Her poetry is a living testimony to the power of words and the possibility of freedom through them. She is an important addition to this collection of voices and proof of the power and eternity of words that cannot be silenced.

If words have been the patrimony of men, and above all, if access to words is of more transcendence than the words themselves, then women's writing, created in a new territory and still discovering new ways of making poetry, represents a highly experimental and unusual form of expression. The section "The Moon's Cadaver" incorporates the voices of poets who have attempted to create a new vision of women and words. These are women who write poetry with a lyricism and a language structure that are both unusual and diversified. Chilean Cecilia Vicuña is obsessed with constructing a new way of writing poetry, of uniting fragments and objects through conjunctions and through the elaboration of well-arranged, pre-fabricated words. Her poetry, which reflects a gaze filled with beauty and seduction, implies a new configuration, as well as the constant knowledge that language is the legacy of women. Argentinian Alejandra Pizarnik has a prominent place in this section with texts from *The Book of Diana* and others. Here we can appreciate with absolute clarity the search and the transgression of the poem and the image it elicits:

> *I jumped from myself to dawn*
> *I left my body next to the light*
> *and sang the sadness of being born.*

Elsa Cross, from Mexico, belongs to a group of women who experiment with the various paths that language can follow. Cross, based on her experience in India, creates a descriptive poetry filled with unusual images which approach a post-modernist conception of space and words, making her texts astonishing in their originality and their ability to transport us to distant places. The same thing happens with Jeannette Miller's poetry. One of the Dominican Republic's most distinguished poets, her writing transports the reader to new and vivid landscapes, illuminated and transposed by the powerful images of her skillfully-wrought language. Clara Silva, a precursor of the current generation of poets, also creates a landscape of powerful and gripping images, alternating past and present in unexpected ways. Silva is one of the most fascinating surrealist figures of Uruguay, yet her work is totally unknown in English. The reader will find in the poetry of Rosita Kalina a poetry that relates to a biblical imagery, especially that of the Old Testament. This poetry also has close resonances to the heritage of Spanish mystics like Santa Teresa de Jesus. Kalina is also a poet deeply rooted to the tradition of Jewish mysticism and to the revindication of the lives of the prophets. The poetry of Mexico's Coral Bracho is filled with elements associated with the subterranean, the invisible and the world yet to be born. Also included in this section is the work of the unusual and gifted poet Giannina Braschi, whose work, unlike that of her Puerto Rican contemporaries, is linked to the tradition of the Latin American surrealists like Silva and Pizarnik.

 "Gestures From My Window" is made up of a diverse group

of poets whose poetry is united by deep and powerful reflections on their surroundings and their history which go beyond ties created by gender or nationality. This section shows a preoccupation with issues such as the definition of nation and the exploration of identity as Latin Americans. The poem "Without Histories" by Bolivia's Blanca Wiethüchter exemplifies this vision:

> *We who are responsible for the living*
> *and have been born in the third world*
>
> *We who ask for justice*
> *and live in South America*
>
> *We who die in Bolivia*
> *desolate and alone*
>
> *we are the history that cannot be written*
> *and journey with the head cut off.*

Together with the poems of Wiethüchter are those of Laura Riesco of Peru, who muses on the possibilities of speaking and the deafness that surrounds her. Another similar voice is that of Guatemalan Romelia Alarcón de Folgar. Her poetry incorporates introspective and everyday elements regarding a Christ without history. Words as a call, a challenge or defiance is one of the metaphors that links the poems in this section, as in Riesco's "So You Would Listen to Me":

> *So you would listen to me*
> *I tangled your silence*
>
> *My words became*
> *shrill with the wind.*

We have poems by Magda Portal, founder of the *Arprista* party in Peru, next to poems by Yolanda Bedregal. In their works, which are characterized by a profound lyricism and introspection, they both depict landscapes, love, silence and the cadences of poetry.

The last section of this anthology, "To Be Seventeen Again," contains texts of popular poetry keeping alive the strong oral traditions of the Americas. The poems by Violeta Parra, a singer as well as a writer, have a prominent position within Chile's folklore. In her lyrics, we can appreciate the coming together of diverse elements from traditional lore. "To Be Seventeen Again" and "I Curse the Sky So High" are examples of Violeta Parra's legacy to and about Latin American culture. This section also contains the poems of Pita Amor, the Mexican troubador who still sings in the streets and coffee houses and who, in the 1920s, started the Mexican art gallery where Frida Kahlo first exhibited her work.

Throughout this vast landscape of texts, voices and visions, poetry appears to be a communal act, a way of learning and a way of living. In his acceptance speech for the Nobel Prize for Literature, Octavio Paz said, "Soon I discovered the defense of poetry, disregarded in our century, became inseparable from the defense of liberty." Paz also said that "throughout history and under the most diverse circumstances, poets have participated in politics. I do not refer to poetry as a form of art to be used by the State. No. I refer to the free participation of the poets in the matters of his/her city." Paz's words ring true for the vibrant mosaic of voices this anthology exemplifies. From Chile to Nicaragua, from Mexico to the United States, women poets have written not only to live but to really inhabit themselves in the magic circle of words that matter. They have claimed a space in the Latin American landscape that is very much their own. A space where words are like the magic glow of a paradise.

— Marjorie Agosín
Wellesley College
Wellesley, MA

Translated by Monica Bruno.

Like the Magic Glow of a Paradise

. . . .

Ana Istarú

Costa Rica's Ana Istarú (1954) is considered to be one of the most innovative authors of Latin American poetry, especially for her erotic poems. *La Estación De Fiebre* (1980,) her best-known book, was recognized in 1983 by the "Editorial Universidad Centroamericana." Among her most outstanding works are *Palabra Nueva* (1975) and *Poemas Para Un Día Cualquiera* (1976). Istarú is also an actress and performs with various groups in San José.

. . . .

XV

From where have you come,
sleeping man.
What cloud spilled you,
what caravel.
Who authorized you to scatter
water lilies,
who slid on your skin
the silver bird.
You rest in my bed carelessly
you are a forgotten angel
inside a stateroom.
I do not understand this man
so lengthy.
I cannot sleep now: my sheet
insists on being the trade wind,
the flower of the lavender.
My pillow, that retakes
its trip of sea gulls.
My old shoes, two sea urchins.

And this small man,
naked without even a gardenia.
Why does my hand fly
to his unwary porcelain,
to his quince flesh.
What disappointment.
What will I look at again, never
if only I can look at my visitor.
From where came the bramble of your eyebrows,

the two copper points of your thorax?
What velveteen will I seek,
if not your soft hair.
What vessel, what kiss,
what shore without your mouth,
sleeping man.
What bread of gold
without your dream.

Translated by Shaun T. Griffin and Emma Sepúlveda-Pulvirenti.

XVII

Then
an awakened citron
there in the
faraway country
of an overflowing
crotch.
I caress the
most erect
corner that was
set in your flesh.
How much unveiling
lovingly
your stalks
your anchor of curling moss.
I reach out to you,
I implore you,
I arouse you.
What darkness of rains I carry
in my belly
to braid your long
intensity
of softest steel.
Then
here in the
valley of thighs
the night pushes
back and forth
— sweet teacher —.
My concave texture
drinks up your fruit.
Here in this humble and exact
time,
peak of pleasures

— your fruit that shrinks,
a child destroyed —
the universe stops.

XXVI

Bodies
tidal waves
downy hair dark as night
sweat
lobe tongue
schools of fish
smell
pink openings
now moist
multitudes
upright masts
stamens
but sweat
glossy sweat
bays let loose
glowing end
now
                pink
          pink
pink
endlessly pink.

XXVII

The moon became mired on our bed.
It left this comb, this mother-of pearl, this nectar.
It placed bright silk around your roughness.
It placed fragrant crystal on all the linens
it found and it only found
the winged tuberoses of your back.
The warm one, the thief, the unexpected
came to drink the sleeping sparks of your forehead,
the crumbs of this love that we commit.
The moon became mired on our bed,
that silver onion, that feline version
of the snow, that spoon.
The frightening one, the outlaw
came to steal your bread, your sex of freshest gold
coming from my best
oven. The unexpected one, warm one, thief!
A handful of azaleas.
The outlaw.

Translated by Mary Jane Treacy.

XIX

A crescent moon
rides between my legs.

Your thighs illumine,
steed, the budding sun.

The husband dove,
the round plum.

This wife that I am,
a caracole.

The darkest hare
rises in my wise man.

The horizon dwells in me
with guava and curve.

The axis of his body
of my body is the axis.

An ebony in two bouquets,
a tangled ink.

A crescent moon
rides between your legs.

My thighs illumine,
steed, the budding sun.

XXXI

To the cove of my breasts your forehead will return,
as my hand, tired of turning,
when our death comes to the table
and from death
may a coral kiss descend
to the tablecloth,
and may a paper kiss descend
and a sea descend
to softly tie us
breasts and forehead and hand,
and may life return at last to the silence,
as my shady forehead,
tired of turning.

XXXII

Your penis rolls to the dream
like a blue daisy
where the nets of darkness rest.
Peace
is a dark silk
after love.

Translated by Shaun T. Griffin and Emma Sepúlveda-Pulvirenti.

Dulce María Loynaz

Dulce María Loynaz was born December 10, 1903 in Havana, Cuba. She is the daughter of Cuban general Enrique Loynaz del Castillo, who fought for independence from Spain. Her brother, Enrique Loynaz Munoz (1904-1966) was also a poet. She became a lawyer in 1927, retiring from that profession in 1961. She was an elected member to the National Academy of Arts and Letters (1951), the Cuban Academy of the Spanish Language (1959) and the Royal Academy of the Spanish language (1968). In 1992, she won the Cervantes Prize, the most distinguished literary prize in the Spanish-speaking world.

. . . .

Last Days of Home

(excerpt)

. . .

I have slept and I awaken . . . Or I haven't awakened
and it's still the lacerating dream,
the shoreless anguish and death in pieces.

I have slept and I woke up inside out,
on the other side of the nightmare,
where the nightmare is unmoveable,
unyielding reality.

I have slept and I awaken. Who awakens?
I feel severed from myself,
sucked in by a
monstrous concave mirror.
I feel without feeling and knowing myself,
scattered entrails, unhinged skeleton,
and the other dream I was dreaming, thrashed.
Something swarms over me,
something hurts terribly
and I don't know where.
What buzzards bite into my head?
From what beast is the fang that tears my flesh?
What moonfish buries itself into my side?

Now I swallow the truth whole!
It is men, men who

---

harm me with their weapons.
Men I mothered
without birthing, wife without
fulfillment of the flesh, sister without brothers,
daughter without rebelliousness.

It is the men and only them,
made of better clay than mine,
whose greed was greater
than the need to hold on to me.

I was sold at least,
because I became so worthy in their accounts,
that I was of no worth for their tenderness.
And if for tenderness I'm unworthy, then I'm worth nothing . . .
And it's time to die.

Embrace

Today I've felt the
whole river in my arms . . . I've felt it
in my arms, trembling and alive
like the body of a green man . . .

This morning the river has been
mine: I lifted it out of its ancient
river bed . . . And I took it to heart!
The river weighed greatly . . . The river,
pained, palpitated from being
wrenched apart . . . — Cold fever
of the water . . . : It left a bitter taste
in my mouth, of love and death . . .

The Calm

     The tired river took shelter in the shade
of sweet trees, of the serene
trees that do not need to run . . .
And it stayed there in a bend.

     There's the calm. A bit of root
ties it to the shore of its soul:
As it reflects lights and shadows
it sleeps a sleep without distances . . .

     It's noon: A dove drifts
by the blue sky . . .
The river is so still
that the hawk, hidden in the branches
momentarily doesn't know
where it will sink its claw:
into the fine bird of the air
or into the bird, finer still, of the water . . .

Time

1.

    The kiss I didn't give you
has become a star inside me . . .
To make it come back again
  — and in your mouth — as a kiss!

2.

    To be as the river
fugitive and eternal:
To go, to arrive, to flow
and always be a river, fresh . . .

3.

    It's too late for the rose
It's too soon for winter.
My hour is not found on the clock
I've been left out of time! . . .

4.

    Late, soon, yesterday lost . . .
tomorrow uncrafted, today
uncertain . . . Measures that can't
fasten, hold down a kiss! . . .

5.

    A kilometer of light
a gram of thought
(at night the clock that beats
is the heart of time . . .)

6.

    I'm going to measure my love
with a ribbon of steel
One end into the mountain
The other . . . hammer it into the wind! . . .

Sea Surrounded

The sea is a blue garden of crystal flowers
but the beach is always the scene of death. You are
my beach to die on . . . It is your eyes that surround me,
that break the waves for me. And with the sea in
my arms and an open horizon, I will perish in you,
grey beach of your eyes, the power of one grain joined to another,
moss-covered wall, shield made of wind.

Futile Flight, Futile Fugue

The water of the river goes fleeing from itself:
It is afraid of its eternity.

Snow

Snow is water
tired of running . . .
Snow is water
detained an instant — water at a point
Water emptied of time and distance.

The Cloud

Cloud, journey of water through the sky
Cloud, cradle for child — water,
rocking itself in the air pierced
by birds . . .
Cloud, heavenly infancy of the rain . . .

XXX

Solitude, solitude so sought after . . . I love you
so much, that I'm sometimes afraid that God
will punish me some day by filling my life up with you . . .

Translated by Alan West.

Cristina Peri Rossi

Cristina Peri Rossi was born in Montevideo, Uruguay, in 1941. Active in the left-wing resistance to military oppression in Uruguay, she was forced to flee her native country in 1972 to exile in Barcelona. Her work consists of poetry, fiction, and essays. Among her books are *Descripción de un naufragio* (1975), *Evohé* (1971, English translation 1994), *El libro de mis primos* (1969) and *La nave de los locos* (1984).

. . . .

from *Evohé*

Tired of women
of the terrible stories they told me,
tired of the flesh,
its tremblings and yearnings,
like a hermit,
I took refuge in words.

A woman dances in my ears
words from childhood
I listen to her
calmly look at her
am looking at her ceremoniously
and if she says smoke
if she says fish caught in our bare hands,
says my father and my mother and my siblings
I feel something undefined
slipping from antiquity
a molasses of words
for, while she speaks,
she has conquered me
holding me like this,
hooked to her letters
syllables and consonants
as if I had penetrated her.
She has me hooked
whisering to me ancient things
things I've forgotten
things that never existed

but now, when pronounced,
become facts,
and while she speaks to me she takes me to bed
where I wouldn't want to go
because of the sweetness of the word *come*.

When she opens her mouth and doesn't sigh
but delicately goes threading letters,
an *o* here, an *a* over there,
that fine consonant sharp as a needle,
light as a feather
and when she has finished a pretty phrase
she flings it into the air
and we all line up to watch it
to observe its qualities
for she has so well combined the sounds
the colors
one would think her a poet
laying words out with harmony
making them sound so well
and I think that just like her periods
her shoulders
her breasts must ring
and damned it I don't begin to think on the music
her legs will make
and how her hair will tremble
shaken in the trill
and how her hands will vibrate in the melopoeia
then with an ax I destroy the piano.

to write
to eat
to go to the movies
to listen to any music
to sleep
to keep vigil
to stroll by statues
to set myself up in a house
to get a cat

to buy a much-needed piece of furniture.
to never leave the city,
the country,
naturally, to make poetry,
naturally, to believe in the women,
to love her an entire day
and then, dissatisfied,
to love other women,
to leave her love for another's
to tell stories,
and among those stories,
to tell this story,
to die a few more days,
and perhaps — if we get along well —
to die even some years.

Translated by Diana P. Decker

Delmira Agustini

Delmira Agustini (1886-1914) is one of Uruguay's most venerated authors. She is considered to be one of the most experimental writers, as well as the initiator of erotic poetry in Latin America. Her principle work is *Los Calices Vacios* (1968). She also wrote *El Libro Blanco* (1907) which is considered to be her fundamental text.

. . . .

In Fields of Sleepdreaming

The pack of wild colts went smoking by,
muzzles ferocious, hides hirsute,
manes swept out stiff, bold, like thick staves;
they came through as the fierce North Winds do;

Then they were eagles of varied and somber plumage
bringing grand visions from their peaks;
in the serene flight of their august inspiration,
in the pride of Olympian lineage

they crossed eastward through the translucid
sky; behind them, like a candid host
rising in flight, a dove white as the snow appears.

I can forget the great, egregious bird and the fiery brute
when I think that in the solemn skies of Ideas
what is sometimes lovely, very lovely, is a dove.

To Death, from the Genie of My Poetry

Somber empress,
if one day,
wounded by a strange and salt-sad whim,
I should come to your somber tower
with my feathery and splendid Wise Man baggage

to spill my tribulations into your marble goblet
you must further seal your door, and snuff your candles . . .

In my rare treasure,
among diamonds and golden Topaz
and the great ruby, bloody as an angry wound,
is the flushed and bluish bud of a star
that will open before the suspenseful eyes of Life
like a new, imperishable and lovely light!

Public Prayer

Eros: have you never perchance felt
pity for the statues?
One might think them the stone pupa
of who knows what terrible race
in an eternal, untellable waiting.
The sleeping craters of their mouths
give out the black ash of Silence;
from the columns of their shoulders
flows the copious shroud of calm
and night flows from their orbits;
victims of the Future or of Mystery,
they await life or Death
in fearsome and wondrous cocoons.
Eros: have you never by chance felt
pity for the statues?

Pity for lives
that do not gild your good wealth with fire
or pour forth or unleash your storms.
Pity for bodies robed
in the solemn ermine of Calmness,
from the luminous brows bearing
great marble lilies of purity,
heavy and glacial like blocks of ice;
pity for the ice-gloved hands
that pluck neither

the luscious fruits of the Flesh
nor the fantastic flowers of the soul;
pity for the eyes that flutter
spiritual eyelids:
scales of mystery,
black drop-curtains of rose visions . . .
For all their distant looking they see nothing!
Pity for the tidy hair-shapes
— mystical aureolas —
combed like lakes
that never feel the air of the black fan,
the enormous black fan of the tempest;
pity for the illustrious souls
carved from diamond,
true, tall, ecstatic,
the lightning-rods of moral domes;
pity for lips like celestial settings
where the pearl of the Host
glows invisible;
lips that never were,
lips that never seized upon
a vampire of fire
with greater thirst and greater hunger than an abyss.
Pity for the sacrosanct sexes
armored by Chastity with an astral vine leaf;
pity for the soles of feet drawn
by eternity that drag
the burning sandals of their wounds
through the eternal azure;
pity, pity, pity
for all those lives for whom
the lofty perch of Pride
staves off your wonderful inclemency:

Aim your suns or your rays at them!
Eros, have you never perchance felt
pity for the statues?

The Swan

A blue eye-pupil in my park
is the sentient mirror
of a clear, a very clear lake . . .
so clear, that sometimes I believe
my thought is printed
on its crystalline page.

An air flower, a water flower,
grave and genteel as a prince,
swan is the soul of lake
with two human eye-pupils;
lily wings, rose oars . . .
beak in fire, neck sad
and proud, and the whiteness
and smoothness of a swan . . .

The grave and candid bird
has an evil-working spell;
a carnation posed as a lily,
he transcends flame and miracle . . .
his white wings trouble me
like two torrid arms;

never did lips burn
like his beak in my hands;
never a head fell
so languid in my lap;
never has such lively flesh
suffered or enjoyed:
uncoiled throughout his veins run
filters twice human.

His head is crowned
with the ruby of lust:
and he drags his desire along
in a roseate train . . .

I give him water in my hands
and he seems to drink fire;

and I seem to offer him
the whole vessel of my body . . .

And he lives so in my dreams
and fathoms so in my flesh
that I sometimes wonder if the swan
with his two fleeting wings,
his odd human eyes
and red burning beak,
is only a swan in my lake
or rather a lover in my life . . .

By the edge of the clear lake
I inquire of him in silence . . .
and silence is a rose
on his beak of fire . . .
Yet, it's in his flesh he speaks to me
and it's in my flesh I understand him.

Sometimes I am utterly and only my soul!
Other times I am utterly and only my body!
He sinks his beak inside me
and remains still, as though dead . . .
And on the crystalline page,
in the sentient mirror
of the lake which sometimes
reflects my thought,
the swan is a startling red,
and I am a frightening white!

The Break

Once there was a chain: strong as a destiny,
sacred as a life, sensitive as a soul;
I have cut it with a lily and I go on my way
with the stupendous coldness of Death . . . In calm

curiosity my spirit peers at its inner
lagoon, and the crystal of the sleeping waters
reflects a god or a monster, masked within
a dark sphinx suspending from other lives.

Wild for Love

I am wild for love and suffer a hunger for hearts,
of doves, vultures, deer, lions,
there is no dish more tempting, no flavor more pleasing;
I was done with debauching my instinct and my claws
when upright on an almost other-worldly plinth
I was dazzled by the statue of an ancient emperor.

And I waxed enthusiastic; my desire rose
like fulminous ivy up and about the stone column
to his seemingly snow-nourished chest;
and I shouted at the impossible heart . . . The sculpture
upheld its pure and high-serene glory,
its brow within Tomorrow, and its foot set in the Past.

Undying, my desire holds fast
to the stone column like bleeding ivy.
And since then I have been biting dreamstruck into a
statue's heart, the utmost prey for my lovely claws;
neither flesh nor marble, it is a bloodless,
unfluttering, heatless mass of star . . .
With the essence of a superhuman passion!

Life

It's to you I come in my hours of thirsting, as to
a clear, cool, mild, colossal fountain . . .
And the stinging fire-snakes always die
in the gentle and powerful current.

I come to you in my weariness, as to the shaded woods
in whose deep velvet fatigue falls
sweetly asleep, with breeze music,
bird and brook music . . .
and I always come out of the shaded woods
radiant and spry as a daybreak.

I come to you in my wounds, as to the vessel of balms
in which pain drinks itself to death by oblivion . . .
And I bear away
my wounds, sealed like dead mouths,
and bandaged in delights by your good hands.

When the cold girds me in a painful sweatcloth,
I come to you livid,
as to the golden corner of a home,
as to the sun's universal Home! . . .
And I turn all to roses like a springtime,
clothed in your fire.

It's to you I come in my pride
as to the ductile tower,
as to the single tower –
which will raise me on high over all things!
Over the very summit –
bold and growing –
of my eternal fancy!

You are the only prey!
You are the eternal prey
for my hungry life!
The smell of your blood,
the color of your blood
shiver in my eagles' avid beaks.

I come to you in my desire
as in a thousand devouring abysses, a full-open
uncontainable soul . . .
And you offer it all to me! . . .
Mysterious seas that have blossomed into worlds,
mysterious skies that have blossomed into heavenly bodies,
the heavenly bodies and the worlds!
. . . And the constellations of spirits pending
between worlds and heavenly bodies . . .
. . . And the dreams that live further out than the heavenly bodies,
closer in than the worlds . . .

How am I to quit on you – Life! – ,
how leave the sweet heart
that like a fertile fatherland
is hospitable and giving?

For, to me, the earth,
to me space,
(all spaces!) are the ones
encompassed in the sheer horizon of your arms . . . !
For, to me, what you hold beyond is Death,
simply, prodigiously! . . .

The Sweet Reliquaries

Some time ago a soul, now erased, was mine.
It thrived on my shadow . . . Whenever I so desired
the golden fan of its laughter would open wide,

or its weeping would bleed out another stream;

a soul that I would ripple, like a wealth of hair
spilt into my hands . . . A fire and wax-wrought flower,
it died of one of my sorrows . . . It was so ductile,

so faithful, that sometimes I doubt if it ever really was . . .

The Ineffable

I am dying somehow strangely . . . Life is not killing me,
Death is not killing me, Love is not killing me;
I am dying of a thought as mute as a wound . . .
Have you never felt the strange pain

of an immense thought that takes root in your life,
devouring soul and flesh and yet never blooming?
Have you never borne within you a sleeping star
that burned all through you and never showed its glow?

Pinnacle of Martydoms! . . . To eternally bear
the tragic seed, the wrenching and arid seed,
driven fiercely into your guts like a fang! . . .

Yet to pluck it one day as a flower
that would open miraculous and inviolable . . . Ah,
it would be no greater to have in one's hand the head of God!

Marble Beads

I, the marble statue with fiery head, while
smothering my temples in a cold, white plea . . .

Encase in a gesture like a palm-tree or a star
thy body, that hypnotic alabaster gem
carved in sheer kisses and burnished in its age;
serene, as though having the moon for armor;
white, and more so than were thou the foam of
the Race, and from the tabernacle of thy chastity

send me a snowfall of the deep irises of thy soul;
my shadow will kiss thy mantle of calm
which growing and growing will wrap me in with thee;
then my flesh will be lost in thine . . .
then my soul will fuse with thine . . .
then will glory be . . . And we will be a god!

Grant me this, dear God:
Love of the cold and white
Love of statues, lilies, stars, gods . . .

Shadow Beds

Black beds gain the most potent
rose of love; they take root in death.
Huge outstretched beds of sadness,
knife-carved and canopied
in sleeplessness; parted
curtains bespeak dead falls of hair;
                          like kindred heads
the deep pillows are good:
plinths of Dreaming and steps of Mystery.
If we fall thus to a bed, crying,
like a flower of death, like a potent
fruit ripe with passion, in flesh and soul —
        they shall be desolate, lovely species
that kiss the profile of the stars
treading the soft palm leaves.

— Glory be to somber love,
like death it rots and dignifies:
Do grant me this, dear God!

                                   Translated by Mark McCaffrey.

Idea Vilariño

Idea Vilariño (1920) an outstanding Uruguayan poet and the author of such collections as *Poemas de Amor* (1972), *Nocturnos* (1976), *No* and *Pobre Mundo,* can be characterized as a minimalist in her creative expression. Perhaps best known for her love poems, she is also a highly regarded translator and literary critic.

. . . .

What Was Life

What was life
what
what rotten apple
what scrap
what debris.

It must have been a rose
it must have been
a gilded cloud
that bloomed
delicate
overhead.

It must have been a rose
it must have been
a felicitous flame
or anything at all that's
weightless
free of pain
glad to be
easy
easy.

It couldn't have been just hallways
sordid sunrises
revulsion
dreary chores
routines
deadlines.
It couldn't be
it couldn't.

Not that
what was
what is
the foul street air
winter
the assorted flaws all the
wretchedness
the fatigue

in a barren world.

If I Died Tonight

If I died tonight
if I could die
if I died
if this fierce coupling
endless
merciless contest
pitiless embrace
kiss with no quarter
would build and build and abate
if right now
if now
I were simply to lay down and die
feeling it's over at last
that at last the struggle can cease
and the light were no longer a sheaf of swords
and the air were no longer a sheaf of swords
and the hurt of others and living and love
and all that were no longer a sheaf of swords
and were done with me
for me
forever
and it no longer hurt
and it no longer hurt.

There is no hope

There is no hope
that things will work out
that the pain will let up
and the world settle down.
It's not at all clear that
life will sort out
its chaotic dimensions
its mindless gestures.
There will be no happy end
no kiss everlasting
of rapt surrender
to herald other days.
Nor will there be any
early spring morning
fresh and fragrant
to set out lighthearted.
Instead all the pain
will invade anew
and nothing will be spared
its heavy stain.
We'll have to go on
keep right on breathing
put up with the light
and vilify sleep
cook with no faith
mate with no passion
chew with distaste
forever after with no tears.

No

I shouldn't write this
shouldn't sit here
suffering
feeling
the horror of the void
letting myself
this
become vertigo
nausea.
I really should look away
really should laugh it off
once and for all
let it be.

A Visitor

You're not mine
you're not here
in my life
at my side.
You don't eat at my table
or laugh or sing
or live for me.
We're strangers
you
and I too
and my house.
You don't belong here
you're a visitor
who's after who wants
nothing but a bed
at times.
What choice do I have
giving in to you.
But I live alone.

Maybe Then

Maybe if you saw Hiroshima
I mean Hiroshima mon amour
if you saw
if you spent two hours suffering like a dog
if you saw
how much it can hurt hurt burn
and twist the soul like that iron
strip away joy forever
like charred skin
and you saw that nevertheless
there are ways to go on to live stay around
bearing no visible wounds
I mean
then
maybe then you'd believe
maybe then you'd suffer
understand.

Each Afternoon

Each afternoon draws to a close
beautifully dies
and each of us
each of us?
admires that beauty knowing
knowing?
it's yet one more that's dying
yet one more that's running out
yet one more that's slipping away
yet one more that never again
one more
one less.

Lifelong farewell

These days
those others
with their desolate motionless clouds
scent of honeysuckle
rumble of thunder in the distance.
These days
those others
with their radiant air and broad horizons
and a red bird perched on a fence.
These days
those others
this excruciating love of the world
this daily lifelong farewell.

How to shrug off

How to shrug off how
to drive out the bleak
remembrance of death
that corrosive memory
that wound.
Why it's a staggering price
our wondrous pride.

How disgusting

How disgusting
what a disgrace
this anxious creature
clinging to life.

How Awful

How awful
if there were a god
and those two stars
tiny twinkling twins
were the two beady eyes
— malicious
wakeful
mean-spirited —
of god.

Like a Floating Jasmine

Like a floating jasmine
that falls weightless through the air
that falls falls
falls.
What else can it do.

Like a dog howling endlessly

Like a dog howling endlessly
howling hoplessly
at the moon
at death
at its life so short.
Like a dog.

Like that man who kicks off his shoes

Like that man who kicks off his shoes
and sighs
and collapses clothes and all
and never looking
never seeing
stares at the ceiling
with huge vacant eyes.

Translated by Louise B. Popkin.

Clementina Suárez

Clementina Suárez (1902-1991), a prominent poet and feminist, was one of Honduras's most important artistic figures. Among her works are *Engranajes* (1936) and *Corazón Sangrante* (1930).

. . . .

Poem for Mankind and Its Hope

I look now within myself
and am so distant,
budding in hidden spaces,
rootless, no tears, no crying out.
— Complete within myself —
in my own hands,
in the world of tenderness
created by my own flesh.

I have watched myself be born, grow, without a sound,
without branches of aching arms,
subtle, silent, with no words to wound,
nor womb overflowing with fish.

Like a dream-rose my world was fashioned,
Angels of love were always faithful to me
in the poppy, in joy and blood.

Every seashell traced my path
and taught me the moment to arrive.
And I learned to be on time
For my date with water, ash
and despair . . .

Fragile was my tree, but always vibrant
To man and bird I have been constant,
I have loved as the geraniums must,
like children, like the blind.

But on any scale
I was always out of bounds,
because my impeccable and recently new world
chews up old façades,

fashions, and useless habits.

My caress is combat
urgency to live,
prophecy of a demanding sky
that footsteps sustain.

I create the eternal,
within and without me,
in search of my universe.
I learned, arrived, entered,
with full knowledge
that the poet who walks alone
is like a dead man, an exile,
an Archangel who kneels to hide his face,
a hand that drops its star
and denies himself and his people
their acquired or supposed inheritance.

From this blind and absurd death or life,
my world was born,
my poem and my name.
This is why I speak tirelessly of man,
of man and his hope.

Like the Magic Glow of a Paradise

I walked out of my dress
and went to meet my body,
and then I knew
the worth of my feet, my hands, my legs,
my stomach, my sex, my eyes and my face.

I saw the delight that each had given me
and said to myself:
What magic in the circle of my waist,
what new and ancient echoes in the stream of my veins,
what voice in my throat,
what wordless syllable on my lips,
what thirsts have been quenched!
Hurriedly I went out my door
to walk unfettered,
to touch the ground with my feet,
to send blazing arrows from my eyes,
to devour landscapes,
to weave my hands in the hieroglyphics of lightning,
to leave here in my sex
— fertile tree —
the aroma of life.

I have absorbed, breathed, shouted,
live, live, live.
As if I were waking up again and again
a bee busily
sipping its heavenly honey.
Dawn that thrives here in my breast,
Toolmaker working day and night
fulfilling the task.

I throw open
the doors of my house,
scatter the bedclothes.
I look in the mirror, a dwelling
that cannot contain me.
My pale violet ring shines
with delirious purpose,

my lamp, my clock,
held in the shadows of time.

My shoes unnoticed beside the bed
and my features ambling through a dream
like a decoration for a poem
written on the lines of my hand,
or on the metallic flash of my senses,
tulips burning, burning.

My archangel profile
dances with the ray of light,
stops its reflections on my forehead
and tumbles my hair with its fire
like the magic glow of a paradise.

Now That I have Grown Up, Mother

You who knew nothing, understood everything
silent and full you descended to me
spilling over my shores
your calm, serene worlds.
That's why I was able to leave you again and again, ascend,
be strong in life's battle
because I knew I could always
leave the clamour behind
and come home,
to the ageless root of your tenderness
where I was but a little girl
safe in your love.
Now I have grown up, Mother,
and despair licks at my heart,
the cold sweat of fear
paralyzes my eyes.
Dressed in blood, in night,
I spell your deepest name
naked and bright today in death.

Another Poem to My Mother

Mother:
Only hours after your death
your house is no longer mine.
Sitting at the door
I looked inside,
where pain began to stain everything
and fear beckoned me from the darkness.
I walked barefoot, so as not to waken you
and delay your journey.
I dressed as a child the more quickly
to trace your steps.
I put the years behind me
to eat bread from your hands,
like a wounded animal I shivered from the cold,
Where, I cried, can I rest my head now
heavy with dreams?

When I was a child
I wept in your skirts.
Now death has stolen
my nightingale, my motherland,
my mistress, my madonna.
I haven't the spirit to eat these apples,
nor birds to nest in my breast,
I am an orphan and most definitely alone,
now I could sleep in the street
crying and moaning
inconsolably.
But perhaps it is your face that looks at me
from within, and holds fast
to my heart in the night.

The Poem

If you start to write a poem
think first of who will read it.
Because a rhyme is only a rhyme
when someone understands it and it lives on
over and above all,
having escaped the mediocrity
that flippancy or wordiness exalts.

A poem is not necessarily as it is
but as it should be in its spirit of justice.
A word is sufficient to love hope
and to speak of this is more important
than the most beautiful but ordinary poem.

A Worker Dies

I will not go down like an old rag
not a single tooth has fallen from my mouth.
My flesh is intact
my head raised high above my supple form.

I will die, but with a fresh mouth
with a firm, clear voice I will answer the call.
I know life's minutes are numbered
that destiny never turns back.

I am not afraid to enter the shadow
let no one come to mourn my death,
the froth of my blood is used up like oil
for that moment I ask only for silence.

Once I am dead I do not want them to fix my hair
or cross my hands over my breast,
I want to be left as I fell
placed simply in the open earth.

I do not want them to dress me up, or to profane my death
by being present those who never were in life.
Sincere comrades, those I've always had,
let only them bury me.

Nor do I want a tombstone or a cross,
I want nothing the poor do not have.
Even after my death my fist will be clenched
and my name will be like a flag in the wind.

Translated by Janet N. Gold.

Julia de Burgos

Julia de Burgos (1914-1953) is one of the most venerable figures in Puerto Rican poetry, as well as in cultural identity. She lived a life of exile, traveling between Puerto Rico, Cuba, the Dominican Republic and New York. Among her works, *El Mar y Tú* (Río Piedras, 1981), *Antología Poética* and *Obra Poética* (1961) stand out, the latter containing the majority of her works.

. . . .

Transmutation

I am simple like the light . . .
Nothing tells me as much as your
                            name repeated from mountain
                                                to mountain
by an echo without time that
                    begins in my love
and wheels to the infinite . . .

                    (You . . . !)
                    Almost dove raised
                    on a world of wings
                    that my spirit has created).

You overpower everything for my light.
I am a simple detail in unchanging dawns
loving you . . .

No angry wind seduces my rest
of tendernesses flowing and contracting
between your hand
and my sob.

An affluence of birthing rivers, and silent nightingales
work against me
there where your soul tells my heart
the lightest word.

My feet go detached from yellow tracks
and scale tireless roofs of butterflies
where the sun, without knowing it,

has seen a morning
lightless . . .

To love you
I have detached the world from my shoulders,
and have remained desert in sea and star,
simple
like the light.

Here there is no geography for hands nor spirit.
I am over the silence and in the very silence
of a transmutation
where nothing is shore.

Poem of My Sleeping Sorrow

With closed eyes, full of intimate voices,
I detain myself in the century of my sleeping sorrow.
I watch it in its dream . . .
It sleeps its sad night
detached from the soil where it uproots my life.
Now the gentle career of my soul is not disturbed
nor does it rise up to my face in pain of pupils.

Enclosed in its form
it no longer projects the sensitive line of its fingers
overthrowing my happiness
nor disrupts rhythms
in the perfect harmony of my precious song.

Time no longer leaves me . . .
It sleeps its sad night
from the moment when
you anchored yourself in the light of my rhymes.

I remember that hours rolled themselves empty
on my living sorrow,
when your shadow ran among strange shadows
appropriated by smiles.

My feeling was waiting . . .
But I had moments of crazy suicide.
You delayed so long,
and strong was the music that your echo brought!

I remember that you arrived elemental of instincts.
You also of the centuries the wide sorrow drank;
but you were much stronger, and in powerful strength,
you unearthed your anguish and put mine to sleep.

Poem Arrested at Daybreak

No one.
I went along alone.
No one.
Painting the dawn with my singular color of solitude
No one.

Repeating myself in all the desperations
Silencing within me the cry of searching for you.
Adding up ideals in each broken truth
Wounding the ears of grain with my affliction of raising you up.

Oh absent one!
How I injected my soul in the blue to find you!
And so, consummately crazy
my eyes boiling in the reddest light to possess you,
How I followed the flight of my emotion most covetous
through the host's golden twilights

Until one morning . . .
one night . . .
one afternoon . . .
I stayed like a curled up dove
and I found my eyes through your blood.

Early mornings of gods
marvelously awakened my valleys.
Indifferences!
River-beds!
Swallows! Stars!
Hard dawns and agile.

Everything in you:
wild sun!

And I?
— A simple truth to love you . . .

I Have Lost a Verse

Swallowing the dark truths at my sides
in the silent night I permitted the loss of a verse.

Each truth implored the statue of words
which quickly engraved my active thought;
and not to belong to everyone with impetus of bird,
through the door which it came ran away my verse.

In it there was no desire to raise up emotions
tired and small expressed at the moment,
and dragging life, undid its brief age
and removed itself from the verbal world of my brain.

It left silently, deformed and mutilated,
carrying in its muteness the vague feeling
of having dressed in flesh wasted by words
to exhibit my entrance as a poetic attempt.
         You! Verse!
                  In you is made the life of another mind,
of another strange anxiety, of another pain.
                                      You! Verse!
I have here the great scenario which in your look of bird
deformed and mutilated by not entering in my eaves,
you will see rise up, on shaft of dumb horizons
disappearing below knowing themselves small:

Four streets of men. Four streets square
deeds of the outside sun with impulse toward the inside.

Believers taciturn moving themselves twisted
in the static of four right angles.

Value of water stanched in the not being of centuries
that died of inertia beneath its own weight.

Value of man squared cowering humble
to drown himself in the waters with torpor of slave.

         You! Verse!

In you man did not make himself; nor the centuries.
The static has broken itself in your song.

You! Verse!

You have returned to the vibrant definition of form
that you warmed at the shadow of the first impulse.

Now I can define you. You bring impetus of idea,
and in your words vibrates the rhythm of the new.

You are the today of the world: the affirmation; the strength.
Revolution that breaks the curtain of time!

In your Being, inevitable revolution of the world,
I have found myself on having found my verse.

The Sea and You

The course of the sea over my entry
is blue sensation between my fingers,
and your impetuous leap through my spirit
is not less blue, it births me eternally.

All the color of the dawn awakened
the sea and you swim to find me
and in the madness of loving me till destruction
go breaking the harbors and the oars.

If I had a boat of seagulls,
for only an instant to detain them,
and shout to them my voice so that they beat themselves
in a simple duel of mystery!

That one in the other finds its own voice,
which tie their dreams in the wind
which bind stars in their eyes
which might give, unified their brilliance.

That it might be a duel of music in the air
the magnolias opened by their kisses,
that the waves dress themselves in passions
and the passion be covered by sails.

All the color of the dawn awakened
the sea and you extend it in a dream
that carries my boat of seagulls
and leaves me in the water of the heavens.

Translated by Heather Rosario Sievert.

Carlota Caulfield

Carlota Caulfield is a Cuban-Irish poet who is a professor at Mills College, Oakland, CA. She is the author of several collections, among them *El tiempo is una mujer que espera, Thirty-Four Madrid Street and Other Poems,* and *Angel Dust.* Her most recent book, *Visual,* is a word and sound game. Among other awards, she has won the International Prize Ultimo Novicento and received an honorable mention in the awards given by the Mexican journal *Plural.*

. . . .

In My Labyrinth (The Minotaur's Game)

I.

I have constructed a labyrinth without a Minotaur,
without Daedalus' plans,
without Ariadne,
but Theseus I do have
— at my side —
and I need no magic threads
to discover my passion.

II.

I've constructed a labyrinth
— without Minotaur —
without Daedalus
without Ariadne.
All alone I found the path
that made my love you,
Theseus.

III.

Seemingly, I am Daedalus
and I hide the labyrinth's plans
under the pillow
so that neither Ariadne
      nor Theseus
      nor any other

can discover that I am the Minotaur.

IV.

I've discovered the labyrinth
where the Minotaur takes his siesta
and I need thank neither Ariadne
for her golden thread, nor Daedalus for his idea,
only you, Theseus, do I bless
for having let me voyage
under the wings of your ship.

V.

Tell me, Theseus,
if you still love me:
I, who am no Amazon
nor have the secret
of the labyrinth.
I only want to know
if magic can transform distances.

VI

I have no wings of wax,
I'm not an inventive sorceress,
but in Love,
I too,
Theseus,
am more Ariadne than she herself,
more Minotaur than the labyrinth.

VII.

I was looking at the beach,
and saw the crests of your ship
with my oracle on them:
Yes, I would betray
my race
my all, for your love,
Theseus.

For Albert, the Terrible

I own Pandora's box
so full of infinite blessings;
Time stopped
in an opening in the lid
and I indulge myself
by touching your hands when I wish.

The back-streets of the city
are sleeping under old birds,
and the café Zum Storchem
dampens my lips again,
when those blue espadrilles
bought in the Flohmarkt
create a vibration in nothingness.

Albert, what beauty in those eternal
eyes of yours,
which play, which tell,
which love, which infinitely surprise.

That three Guinnesses enjoyed
under the portraits of Joyce,
and Laberknödel Zwiebelsauce, spätzli
in the Bierhalle Kropf Zürich
of Samstag. 13. Juni. 1981,
two days before my going into Hell.

Albert, on opening my goat's skin
one day,
I found your goat's skin
coming out from inside of me.

You All Know the Story of the Two Lovers

Today Eurydice played
With the labyrinthine earth
And imagined herself
Bound to Orpheus' skin
Imagined herself . . .
Somewhere inside him.

Today Orpheus played
With his hands
And imagined himself
Playing a drum
Somewhere inside
Eurydice's intermittent city.

Merci Bien, Monsieur

I see you every morning with a poet's eyes:
a little child takes a walk through the forest,
he picks mushrooms to take to his mother.
He hears a sound. He gets scared and hides.
But he smiles after noticing the unicorn
among the foliage.

Everyday, I love you,
I see behind your Jewish eyes
and capture pieces of forgotten stories.
I see that painting of Vermeer you like so much.
I catch the devil's disease
and fly like Chagall.

From that first day, I looked at your face and heart.
A child keeps a piece of bread under his pillow.

Translated by Chris Allen and Carlota Caulfield.

These Are Not Sweet Girls

. . . .

Perla Schwartz

Perla Schwartz, born in Mexico City in 1955, belongs to the genera-
tion of young Mexican authors. She is also a literary critic and has
written a biography about Rosario Castellanos, *Mujer Que Sabe Latin
Mexico* (1987) and the poetry collection *La Mujer del Camaléon*
(1992). She is the editor of the cultural pages of *El Sol de México*.

. . . .

Snapshots of the Chameleon Woman

Thousands of women hold me
women who spring up
behind the daily disencounter.
Women who support me
behind disorderliness and the void.
Accompanied by them
I cross the shifting asphalt,
I search for an alibi to despair.

I will pretend
I will disguise myself
as a virgin dressed in snow.
I will float before the gazes
and walk slowly toward them.
Everyone will agree
the official scene,
the holocaust of solitude will begin.

Blessed are
the housewives
who control the reins
of their territory
and don't dirty themselves
with dust that is foreign to their furniture.
Blessed are
the housewives

with husbands who subsidize them
and buy them those sticks
that keep them
excessively straight
and with a pious
unmistakable smile.
Blessed are
those who base their tribulations
on the fellow who dared
to stand up to Mariquita
those who are distressed
by the bloody finger of the butcher.
Blessed are they
because they don't question themselves beyond
the fingernail polish,
the nylons that run
or the child who cries in B flat major.

Those who are unfamiliar
with the lengthy disillusionment,
the grief that comes
from fighting tooth and nail,
from searching for
the here and now
before sunset
cannot possibly
light that lantern
beneath which begins
the dance of the belles-lettres.

Today I will not bother
to cook small succulent dishes
or mend the torn blouse.
Today,
I prefer to sit near the window
to wear out my quota of boredom.

I passed the exam
and have pleased everyone.
I am the happily married
woman who lives in glamour
among elegant and well-shaped
wooden furniture
and a smell of vanilla
that penetrates the walls of the house.
The happily married woman
clinging to a husband
stuck to her petticoats
and to a son joined to her breast.
Minimal is the space
that opens in the hours
of a vertiginous dream
that evaporates
like those luxurious perfumes
with which the married woman
adorns herself
while paying credit cards in bulk
which she signs,
justifying her solitude as an excessively useful object.

Marriage is more lonely than solitude
                    –Adrienne Rich

      The house is silent.
Only the voices of the objects can be heard.
The water,
the refrigerator,
the stove.
The window closes.
No one visits the house.
Everyday
the dust conquers the debris.
Two people live in the house
at different times
in different spaces.
Two shadows that wander aimlessly

and project themselves against the wall.
At night,
each one occupies its place beneath
the folded sheets.
When the house is left without inhabitants,
solitude:
a dense net amid the furniture.

      I wash my face,
the masks, and familiar
and foreign gestures remain outside.
The eyes surrender and
the mouth forgets
the smile that disturbs.
The water runs
the artifices dissolve.
The mirror and a foreign image.
Time to abandon the pretenses.
Time to yield to the shampoo and the cold cream,
time to permit the asphyxia
to invade the bedroom.
When morning arrives
the make-up
will occupy the face
once again.
No one will know what has happened.

      I distance the tedium.
Decide to dress myself in red,
exile phantoms
and surround
the uncertainty of fire,
that long restrained desire.
Sleeping skin
does not revive
not in the rain
nor in the silence
that looks out behind the large door.

My body seethes
with an unaccustomed intensity
that emerges from the bones.
You drive away
the smoke at a distance,
you avoid the signs
the bonfire
ungratefully surprised.

Translated by Celeste Kostopulos-Cooperman.

Anabel Torres

Anabel Torres, born in Bogotá Colombia in 1948, is without a doubt one of the most vital voices of Colombian poetry. She has won several national poetry contests and has published *La Mujer del Esquimal* (1980) and *Las Bocas del Amor* (1985). Her work has been translated into German.

. . . .

The Eskimo's Woman

She,
the eskimo's woman
left you this legacy:

snows
wastelands

       and this little well boiling with tears
       thirty meters deep.

A Small Miracle

If only a small miracle
occurred,
if the cook
slipped out of her horrible uniform
like a tired
trickle
leaking from the faucet,

and on the pavement
at midnight
a taxi were waiting for her.

These Are the Sweet Girls

These are
        the sweet girls
                who go to the matinée

These are
the sweet girls
prepared to be the echo,
prepared to be the small round pebble in the center
stirring the concentric
circles
while the waves move further and further away.

These are
the girls with smooth
skin
and a soul
even smoother and,
                        without curves.

Kettle Rooted to the Void

Blowing softly over his eyelashes
life seemed like another.
Today I don't remember the shade of the
                        slow yellow sheets,
and if the waves seemed to me like clapping hands,
or if on the contrary
I had time to feel their monotonous forms.

Dans un bateau
j'étais avec un homme
qui a disparu en pleine mer.

French,
everything is lost and now remains.
Now I am
a woman
rooted to life like a kettle,
        a kettle rooted to the void.
Be that as it may, everything that I touch
blossoms

Smash Your Fist

Kneeling
in this store window
with no other window to arrange,

the passers-by
stay gazing at my cow gaze,

and don't lick me
on their way back.

Merciful
world
smash your fist
against this glass

free me to graze
on unvigilant eyes.

Warmness

I knew how to make myself feel
more than anything
in absence:

I don't know very well
why
but it was warm

A bird sad about flying;

a bird nevertheless.

Translated by Celeste Kostopulos-Cooperman.

Rosario Castellanos

Rosario Castellanos' work can be considered to be one of the most intense and prolific within the panorama of Hispanic American poetry and feminist culture. Castellanos, in her novels, short stories and poetry, expresses the situation of the Latin American woman, of her culture and identity. In her work there is also a profound concern for the indigenous. Among the works of Castellanos are *A Rosario Castellanos Reader* (1987), and *The Selected Poems of Rosario Castellanos* (1988, Graywolf Press).

. . . .

Speaking of Gabriel

Like all guests my son got in the way
taking up a space that was my space,
existing at all the wrong times,
making me divide each bite in two.

Ugly, sick, bored,
I felt him grow at my expense,
steal the color from my blood, add
clandestine weight and volume
to my way of being upon the earth.

His body begged for birth, begged me to let him pass,
allot him his place in the world,
and the portion of time he needed for his history.

I agreed. And through the wound of his departure,
through the hemorrhage of his breaking free,
the last I ever felt of solitude, of myself
looking through a pane of glass, also slipped away.

I was left open, an offering
to visitations, to the wind, to presence.

Parable of the Unfaithful Wife

Before, whenever I talked to myself, I used to say:
if I am what I am
and if I make space in my body and my years
for the process
that the seed permits the tree
and the stone allows the statue, I will be complete.

And perhaps it was true. One truth.

But, oh, I woke as docile as ivy
clinging to a wall just as all lovers
cling to each other with their promises.

And then, solid as an oak, standing tall,
I would spread all around me
the rustling solitude, the welcoming shade,
and I gave the wanderer –
to his knife sharp with memory –
the faithful witness of my bark.

My bitterness was sometimes rest
and sometimes ecstasy,
grace or rage, always the two opposites
ready to annihilate each other
and to rise from the ruins of the vanquished.

Every hour I replaced someone; every hour
I left a dismantled tavern
where I hadn't found even a sputtering candle
and could leave nothing behind.

I usurped names, crowned myself with them so as
to hurl them from me later.

Here I am now, at the end, and I still
don't know how I'll face death.

Silence Around an Ancient Stone

I sit here with all my words intact,
as if with a basket of green fruit.

The fragments
of a thousand ancient toppled gods
seek each other in my blood, hold each other captive, eager
to repair the statue.
From their broken mouths,
a song rises to my mouth,
smell of burnt resin, gesture
of hard-worked mysterious rock.
But I am oblivion, betrayal,
a shell that didn't even hold
an echo of the sea's last wave.
I don't look at the submerged temples;
I look only at the trees whose vast shade moves
above the ruins and whose acid teeth gnash
the wind as it streams by.
And the signs shut themselves beneath my eyes like
a flower in a blind man's clumsy grasp.
But I know: behind
my body crouches another,
and all around me many breaths
cross back and forth
furtive as jungle animals at night.
Somewhere, I know,
exactly like
a cactus in the desert,
a starry crown of thorns
awaits a man just as the cactus awaits rain.
But I know only certain words
in the language or stone
beneath which they buried my ancestor alive.

The Return

I walk the land of Anahuac which is the land of my dead.

Yes: as their names suggest — and other signs —
they are dead. They do not speak.

Some, the most recent, have their chins tied
with the final kerchief.
Others with their jaws intact, calcium reverted
to its mute mineral state.

So, then, do not ask me
to live for them.
To see the world they do not see, to body
forth a destiny left incomplete.

If I need justification
for existing, for doing
and, above all, for not erasing myself
(which would be logical based on the evidence)
I will have to obtain it some other way.

From the living, who turn their backs on me,
who do not see me but who if they did
would reject me like those who know
that, by a law of nature, fewer bodies mean
more space and air and hope?

From those who arrive with the grenade already poised
to explode between their hands?
From those who see in me an obstacle, a ruin,
a hideous sight
that must be destroyed in order to construct the new?

No. The answer will not
come from humans alone.

Perhaps to undertake some great work . . .
Work? Change nature's face?
Add some book to the bibliographies?

Change the course of history?

But that's a man's job — again —
cut to time measured to fit men
following the criteria
they use to accept or reject.

Then what? God? His reign?
It is too late now to invent
or return to golden childhood.

Just accept the facts: you are here
and it's all the same as if you had stayed or never
left. The same. For you. For everyone.

Superfluous here. Superfluous there. Superfluous
exactly like each and every one
you see and do not see.

No one is necessary
not even for you, who by definition
are so needy.

Meditation on the Threshold

No, throwing yourself under a train like Tolstoy's Anna
is not the answer,
nor hastening Madame Bovary's arsenic
nor waiting for the angel with the javelin
to reach the parapets of Avila
before you tie the kerchief to your head
and begin to act.

Nor intuiting the laws of geometry,
counting the beams in your cell
like Sor Juana. The answer is not
to write while visitors arrive
in the Austen living room
nor to lock yourself in the attic
of some New England house
and dream, the Dickinson family Bible
beneath your spinster's pillow.

There must be some other way whose name is not Sappho
or Mesaline or Mary of Egypt
or Magdalene or Clemencia Isaura . . .

Another way of being free and human.

Another way of being.

Poetry Is Not You

Because if you existed
I'd have to exist too. And that's a lie.

There is nothing more than ourselves: the couple,
two sexes reconciled in a child,
two heads together, not contemplating each other
(so as not to turn either one into a mirror),
but staring straight ahead, at the other.

The other: mediator, judge, equilibrium
of opposites, witness,
knot in which what was broken is retied.

The other, muteness that begs a voice
from the one who speaks
and demands the ear of the one who listens.

The other. With the other
humanity, dialogue, poetry, begin.

Origin

I am growing on a woman's corpse,
my roots wrap themselves around her bones
and from her disfigured heart
a stalk emerges vertical and tough.

From the bier of an unborn child:
from her womb cut down before the harvest
I rise stubborn, definitive,
brutal as a tombstone and sad at times
with the stony sadness of the funeral angel
who hides a tearless face between his hands.

Destiny

We kill what we love. What's left
was never alive.
No one else is so close. What is forgotten,
what is absent or less, hurts no one else.
We kill what we love. Enough of drawing a choked breath
through someone else's lung!
There is not air enough
for both of us. And the earth will not hold
both our bodies
and our ration of hope is small
and pain cannot be shared.

Man is an animal of solitudes,
a deer that bleeds as it flees
with an arrow in its side.

Ah, but hatred with its insomniac
glass eyes; its attitude
of menace and repose.

The deer goes to drink and a tiger
is reflected in the water.

The deer drinks the water and the image. And becomes
— before he is devoured — (accomplice, fascinated)
his enemy.

We give life only to what we hate.

The Farewell

Let me speak one word, muzzle,
to say goodbye to what I love.
The earth escapes, flies like a bird.
Its flight draws round wakes in the air,
fresh tracks of aromas and signs of trills.

Everything travels on the wind, ravished.

Ah, to be a kerchief,
only a white kerchief!

Translated by Magda Bogin.

Giovanna Pollarolo

Giovanna Pollarolo (1955) is one of the young and innovative poets from Peru. *Entre Mujeres Solas* (1991) is her first published text.

. . . .

When We Met Again

What would we talk about before? I ask; what of, when we had
neither children nor husband nor maid?
When it was not neccessary to hide nor embellish a well placed,
almost expensive, mask.
We would talk, then, of the future
each would dream of that which today she is not
or of what she has become, though different
to marry, have children
leave home, which resembled a prison
say goodbye forever to the nuns
life like a postcard, without dirty clothes
nor dishes to do
those things which we do not dream even in dreams.

S.L.A.M.

The future of which we dream
is written in ornamental letters
flowers and hearts, drawings allusive to the question
to marry a millionaire
be an actress
model, world famous singer
executive secretary
business woman

judge, lawyer, doctor
even minister, I dare not stop
to gather a fortune
travel
find my prince charming
to be happy and eat partridge
we identify the protagonists
Not at all!, we would say, chuckling
some came near, few
but what they achieved does not glitter
the others are stunned
their dreams have been forgotten at the blink of an eye.

The Sunny Afternoon Dream

Sunny afternoons
he lying on his bed, without shoes
error eliminated
the radio at full blast
she irons and mutters
. . .
I swear when I am older
I won't be like her
and he, he whom I don't yet know
won't be like him
in my days there will be no irons
nor soccer nor sorrow
On Sunday afternoons
only the announcer has a voice
he lives for the passion of soccer
both having forgotten love
she only mutters
I dream of my Glory Sundays.

They All Think

that I'm lucky
I've told them that every morning
I wave goodbye
from the window, with a smile
. . .
I never wait in vain
never a sigh, a concern
but sometimes at dawn
I spy
the coming and going of the people, the street
. . .
I'm lucky, I know
but I'm bored.

The Grocer's Dream

and when they would ask

what are you going to be when you grow up
and without thinking, I would answer
wait on people in a store just like this one
and they would laugh at such a meager dream
they hadn't travelled so much
so the granddaughter would end up, like them
behind the counter.
And they would send me off to study, because one who studies
even if she's a woman, succeeds.

At Breakfast

she is pale, her eyes baggy
a fixed gesture of loathing
has engrained deep lines
the scream, the apprehension
the tight jaw
lips almost non-visible
she used to have an open smile and soft skin
big and beautiful eyes
but she has three children
and a husband for whom she cries
she looks like a withered flower
he, mature and handsome
looks at himself in the mirror and smiles, pleased
who would have thought . . . , as he caresses himself
the ugly duckling.
he's been heavily rewarded
and when he sees her in the mornings
at breakfast
he feels the pleasure of revenge
and a bit of pity.

A Good Marriage

The perfect couple
intelligent, in love
each one shined in his or her own way
he was at the top of the wave
she waited on the dock
"it is not good for the woman to be more than her man"
others would say
"behind every great man there is a great woman"
she would smile

During Recess

we knew no other jobs
we never sang
doctors
lawyers
actress
poetess

Foretold Futures

The reverend mothers
the reverend father
the whole community
of the daughters of Santa Ana
never tired of repeating to us
that we were the future
the wives and mothers of tomorrow
the wives and leaders of the country
the mothers of the future leaders
of the country
God has chosen us
that was the privilege!
for such a great and arduous task.

While My Father

While my father prospered
and my grandmother smiled, pleased
for the well chosen country
being Italian and white was more than enough
was worth more than she ever dreamed
was worth more than money itself
. . .
and there were already grandsons who would go to college
granddaughters who would be teachers
and would marry the sons of the compatriots
who had come from afar, like her
who also prospered and made the city theirs.
There, far away, things happened
the world seemed plagued
but nothing would bother her
here we were in peace.

A Man Went to See the Doltons

A man is approaching
carrying two stones in each hand
he waves them at my face, and chides
"to eat," "to eat"
I run so he will not catch up with me

Lima. Winter. 1990.

In My Days

In my days it seems like a dream, like fiction
right turned wrong
the world was not so far
and my grandmother took her paradise with her.
Those of us who are somebody today, were nothing before
we forgot a language, a country, relatives,
there, we are the Peruvians
and here, like my grandmother from the old world used to say,
everything has become a *zafarrancho*.

Translated by Marjorie Agosín.

Adélia Prado

Adélia Prado (1936), one of Brazil's most distinguished poets, has published six books of poetry, including *Cacos para um vitral* (1980), *O Coracão Disparado* (1977) which won the prestigious Jabuti Prize in 1978, and three books of prose. Her most recent work in English is the *Alphabet in the Park* published by the Wesleyan University Press in 1990. She works as a cultural liason in her native city of Divinopolis.

. . . .

Murmur

Sometimes I get up at daybreak, thirsty,
flecks of dream stuck to my nightclothes,
and go look at the children in their beds.
Right then what I'm most sure of is: we die.
It bothers me not to have coined the wonderful phrase
at cock's crow. The children go on snoring.
Fragments, in sharp focus: his hands
crossed on his chest like the dead,
that little cut on his shoulder.
The girl today so intent on a new dress
is now fast asleep, oblivious,
and this is terribly sad
after she told me: "I think it would be even better
with a ruffle!" and cracked a half-smile,
embarrassed by so much happiness.
How is it that we mortals get bright-eyed
because a dress is blue and has a bow?
I take a sip and the water is bitter,
and I think: sex is frail,
even the sex of men.

Time

To me —who since childhood went on my way
as if my destiny were the exact destiny of a star —
incredible things make their appeal:
paint your nails, expose your neck,
bat your eyes, drink.
I take God's name in vain.
I've discovered that in time
they will make me cry and forget.
I'm twenty years plus twenty,
a western woman who, if I were a man,
would love to be named Eluid Jonathan.
At this exact moment on the twentieth of July,
nineteen hundred and seventy-six,
the sky is thick, it's cold, I am ugly,
I just got a kiss in the mail.
Forty years old: I don't want a knife
or even cheese —
I want hunger.

Heart's Desire

I'm no matron, mother of warriors, Cornelia,
but a woman of the people, mother of children, Adelia.
I cook and I eat.
Sundays I bang the bone on the plate to call the dog
and toss out the scraps.
When it hurts, I yell ouch,
when it's good, I'm brutish,
sensations beyond control.
But I have my crying spells,
little clarities behind my humble stomach,

and a booming voice for hymn-singing.
When I write the book bearing my name
and the name I will give it, I'll bring it to a church,
to a tombstone, to the wilderness,
to cry and cry and cry,
elegant and odd as a lady.

Serenade

Some night under a pale moon and geraniums
he would come with his incredible hands and mouth
to play the flute in the garden.
I am beginning to despair
and can see only two choices:
either go crazy or turn holy.
I, who reject and reprove
anything that's not natural as blood and veins,
discover that I cry daily,
my hair saddened, strand by strand,
my skin attacked by indecision.
When he comes, for it's clear that he's coming,
how will I go out onto the balcony without my youth?
He and the moon and the geraniums will be the same —
only women of all things grow old.
How will I open the window, unless I'm crazy?
How will I close it, unless I'm holy?

Successive Deaths

When my sister died, I cried a great deal
and was quickly consoled. There was a new dress
and a thicket in the back yard where I could exist.
When my mother died, I was consoled more slowly.
There was a new-found uneasiness:
my breasts were shaped like two hillocks
and I was quite naked.
I crossed my arms over them when I cried.
When my father died, I was never again consoled.
I hunted up old pictures, visited acquaintances,
relatives, who would remind me of how he talked,
his way of pursing his lips and of being certain.
I imitated the way his body curled
in his last sleep and repeated the words
he said when I touched his feet:
"Never mind, they're all right."
Who will console me?
My breasts fulfilled their promise
and the thicket where I exist
is the genuine burning bush of memory.

Easter

Age
is a way of feeling cold that takes me by surprise
and a certain acidity.
The way a dog curls up
when the lights go out and people go to bed.
I divide my day into three parts:
the first to look at photographs,
the second to look in mirrors,
the third, and longest, to cry.
Once blonde and lyrical,
I am not picturesque.
I ask God
on behalf of my weakness,
to abbreviate my days and grant me the face
of an aging, tired mother, a good grandmama,
I don't care which. That's what I aspire to
in my impatience and pain.
Because there's always someone
smack dab in the middle of my happiness saying:
"Don't forget your overcoat!"
"You wouldn't have the nerve!"
"Why aren't you wearing your glasses?"
Even a dried rosebud with its powdery perfume —
I want something sweet like that,
something which says: that's her.
So I won't be afraid of posing for a picture,
so I'll be handed a poem on parchment.

Translated by Ellen Watson.

Alicia Galaz Vivar

Alicia Galaz Vivar is a Chilean poet from Valparaíso who currently is professor of Modern Foreign Languages at the University of Tennessee. She has published several books, essays, articles, and poetry collections, among which are *Distant Signs From What is Preferred* (1991), *Craft of Change* (1987), and *Thick Cage for the Female Animal* (1970). She was founder and editor of the poetry journal *Tebaida* (Chile: 1968-1973).

. . . .

Femmemasochism

According to classification born a woman.
Eternal wife to pots, plates, socks,
brooms, kitchens, baby food and flour sifters.
I joy in my apostleship of sheets.
Aseptically I reject ambiguities,
defend the legacy of the spirit,
while exorcizing the budget.

Time's worker, I distribute the thousand and one days
in flagrant compromises, birthdays and baptisms.
A whole web of dropsical behaviors, purgatives.

Loneliness singles me out in the shops and plaza.
In instinct I take refuge.
They control my womb.

They postpone me, limit me, they dose out tenderness
and words.
High level plans condition my every move.
Over giving or not giving birth they
do all the talking.
They create hate and fear.
Throw in my face, laws, religion,
or custom.

And you there smiling, I'll rub you out of Paradise.

Delivery

The round living bulge, more certain today,
knocks on you hard
trying to be born and kicks its heels
into your gut, more than on any day of these past six months
by which you announce its arrival and your heart stirs itself
pulsing with fear.
You would hide yourself but there is no other place,
dread is with you
in the fight for birth whose road has been long
and who stops you on the street
to see your shadow like an inverted poppy
that would have fully matured.
A happy fear was spinning your dream by bucking,
when unseen sounds take shape,
even that of the fly that passes buzzing with summer in its wings
and the watch that unwinds spying.
You persist for the thousandth time in counting the layette
as on normal days
and then rises from your spine the inexorable sign,
purest animal of your blood,
the vulnerable form from the armed fortress
from the hips to the belly like a red blossoming flower
run on the axle of the mill of life.
The inconclusive task of breaking the glass urgently begins again
faithful to its rhythm it is now pain turning
in its ancient grind with the weariness of death.
Your stomach spreads like the underlip of a horse:
they take him by the head
and the solitary breather with triumphal zest
is hanging from your breasts.

Translated by Dave Oliphant.

The Order and the Days

The clear air, the tree's shadow and your shadow,
the order and the days.
Yesteryear's blue rose and the dove of wire.
Your in-tune steps throughout the house,
the mismatched furniture,
the transparent wine of your blood,
the tic-tac of your sleep on another pillow.
to play with marked cards and words
– everything according to the order and the days –
Sunday newspapers, coffee and dense air.
The brown blue rose of the world stripping its petals.
Wasps buzzing hate.
And treachery round and circular like the smoke of your pipe.
You add a black rose to your animal misery,
furiously barren,
emptied of your tenderness in your harsh demand
and, nevertheless,
you are to plant the same crosses and kill the same gods.
Summon deaf death to this, your yellow heart.

Love is Round

Love is round like a seed or an egg,
like the fear of a childhood memory
where you tied hornets by the waist;
just like the game of growing up
among idols of cherry and bread,
with the hands of the clock
keeping the beat of the years
in a drum of bone; however,
as in an undertow, the tide of time
hurls back at you the severed wasps,
and there is no breath, no Spring for death
that surrounds you, round like love.

Femmepoem of Overpopulation

It is not that I seek an eye for an eye or a tooth for a tooth
nor the once upon a time
when the big fish eats the
                                                other one —
or that no one that's rich shall enter paradise
or that it shall be easier for a camel
                        with all its hump on its back
                        to pass through the eye of a needle.
The question is
                who prays
                                        who takes the pill
(the side effects), who aborts, who works
to make the baby grow,
                        who
unites the family during Sunday admonitions.
Who,
     scourer of back rooms,
                                        uses the cleaning cloth,
                                        the infinite cleaning cloth,
and shops and cooks and sweeps and darns and washes and irons
and sews
          and embellishes:
and awaits the absolution of *homo ludens.*
Who swings on the pendulum of offer and demand
Who waits — by night's perfume — for sex
                        and for the appeal.
The questions come out of my mouth
                        or under my sleeve
like cards in a game
                now until the hour
in which modern male: lord of the house
                of the bank
                and of the heavens
erases his smile of better than thou and *homo justus*
washes away the sad fury of mortal decisions.

                                        Translated by Oliver Welden.

Olga Nolla

Olga Nolla was born in Mayaguez, Puerto Rico, in 1938. She studied biology in New York and then returned to the island. She is the author of *Al Sombrero de Plata al Ojo de la Tormenta* (1976), and *Dafne en el mes de Marza.*

. . . .

Erotic Suite

One: This is the way it must be . . .

I don't want to know through whispers if you still love me;
if you still weep through the hours
as you kiss away the memory of my lips
and you pick the flowers from my body
as they resurface in your mind.
I would rather not know.
I want to dream your arms embracing me
in the nocturnal balconies near the sea and the moon.
I want to dream you loving me so I can continue living.
If you no longer remember me
it must be a lie, Calixto.

Two: I have invoked the muses . . .

Since I have not attained
the love of that inexplicable man,
I have invoked the muses.
I love him more now
than when he covered me with his body;
he now covers me with words
and always caresses my breasts and thighs;
our orgasms, slow and measured,
return us to the ancestral call
and inundate us with sweetness
(as San Juan would say . . .)
I read the words of San Juan de la Cruz
and I hear you and see you next to me;

the inexplicable man
who does not want to stop in my port.
But, as you can see, Ulysses,
my fantasy overcomes all obstacles.

Three: In that bar . . .

It was Tuesday and you
soothed your fear with alcohol
– with the merciful help of alcohol –
and then you told me
that you were in love with me.
I thought I was dreaming
and I wanted to awaken, and flee
that prison, flee from that unbearable happiness
which I did not understand.
All around us, other shadows swayed
and the bartender stared,
red-eyed,
between the impenetrable sound, the voices,
hands and arms, lips vibrating
in suspended echoes
while behind the glass
the gods watched, laughingly,
the flapping and the gleam of my tail
and the unmistakable pinkness of my scales:
poor playthings of destiny!
In that rainy bar in Rio Piedras
whose name I don't want to recall:
It was an unbearable happiness . . .
That first time . . .
In which our souls contemplated one another . . .

Four: And all this beauty . . .

Love is a force which moves
spheres,
the energy of the universe.

Philosophers have claimed this
and so have poets and astrophysicists.
I wish I could believe it, even if it were a lie.
My chest swells up
when I imagine a world perched atop the silence:
Rose of lightness, its petals of space,
open its arms with a sigh;
the soul of love unravels
in successive flows;
emanation which transpires softly
through the cores of matter.
I imagine that the cosmos
capsize, weepingly into my two hands.
I imagine that time
looks at me adoringly.
And all this beauty . . .
And all this happiness . . .
Will die with me
if you continue to slight me, Hippolytus.

The Manifest

I love being a woman
to be forty years old
to be mistress of my life
to fall in love with men
to easily forget men
to write my poems
to cook aromatic dishes
to fix exquisite traditional dishes
to talk about hunger with my men
to dress sensually with lace and silks
to undress sensually
to wear red shoes
to grow my hair real long
to paint my toenails
to dream of the novels I plan to write
to see movies made by women
to listen as the rain collides with the air
to listen to thunder
to run the waves in my car inflamed
and to give you the apple, Adam
eat it, eat it.

Thoughts on Innocence

I detest innocent women.
I do not want innocents in my home.
They always force me to tell lies.
They barely know anything about life.
I don't know who would think of protecting them.
It must be men who still long for their childhood.
It must be men who still use slaves.
It must be the most unhappy men I know:
sad patriarchs with their sad customs.
It seems they must think life
is something dirty and evil.
If I ever said long live innocence
it would be after having eaten all
the apples of Paradise.

Greek History

Aristotle said
that we women are mutilated men,
impure beings without souls.
As I heard him I decided to avenge myself
and I wrote on the walls of the city
in big red letters:
Aristotle, faggot
I wrote it many times
until I exhausted my anger
Later, I was overcome by the horror
of the enthroned lie
the fright of my impotence
and the sad historic truth
that my fire had been stolen.

Troubadour Love

A man who loves me
walked past my street today.
He has confessed it many a time
between feeble sighs
and a few tears.
He passed by at the wheel of his car
looking toward my balcony with determination
— It was by chance that I saw him —
— my heart, I suppose, skipped —
Why doesn't he stop his car,
embrace me, steal me away to his castle?
He loves me from afar like Dante to Beatrice,
that's what I figure.
It's a shame I like his mouth, his throat,
his way of looking at the world,
his chest, his presence.
It's a shame I have him sewn to my soul.
If not, I'd say: Stupid man!
You are a coward!
Or I would tell him his love is cruel,
that deep inside, he hates
real women
and only loves, from afar, the ideal woman,
the unattainable . . .
A perfect Provençal troubadour!
Obviously, so much idealism bores.
Besides, it means
that he is not interested in how I feel.
We continue to be imprisoned
within the labyrinths of solitude.
So much love, so many words, and for what?
If only because I could not breathe without his love,
and because he would never understand
I would tell that and more . . .
I suspect all I can do
is cheat on him . . .
Deceive him on purpose
— without him ever knowing —
so as to continue being
his ideal woman.

Reencounter with the Goddess

In order to reach you
I had been baring myself throughout the centuries.
I stripped all I had learned:
Man's laws
and the order of its ire.
And I cursed you again and again . . .
I threw you in the trash.
I broke the delicate threads
of your soul.
And now I rediscover you
living in my mirror.
And I dress in your tunic,
I don your crown of stars.
the rays from your hands,
I remember you standing over the world.
But I will not step on the serpent.
I twist it around my arms,
my powerful arms which give and sever.
And the serpent smiles
because at last I have discovered its secret.

If I Do Not Believe

If I do not believe in God
within me the universe comes to a close.
I touch the thick silence
where neither light, nor any atom,
roams.
I do not fear the silence.
Rather, I feel comfortable.
The skin and the hair, the lips and
the feet of the people I love
seem to me infinitely precious.
A hand over my shoulder produces within me
an uncontrollable joy.
This silence soothes.
I value it, I defend my rights to it:
I confront Medusa face to face,
and I still have not turned into stone.

Translated by Paula Vega.

Paz Molina

Paz Molina was born in Santiago, Chile, in 1945 and is considered to be one of Chile's most provocative poets of her generation. Among her works are *Memorias de un pajaro asustado* (1982) and *Noche Vallejeana* (1992). She now works in for the Neruda Foundation on Isla Negra.

. . . .

Your Anger

Like the brilliance of an eye in darkness
getting closer
I sense your foreboding anger.
A black petal falls, a snake hisses
and my spirit corrodes between your claws.

I'm innocent of the storm
(the gods have sworn to protect me)
but still a bolt of lightning opens spaces.
My charred tree falls.

I belong to you
yet the stone of torment
was someone else's and
the executioner blind.
No. Your hands did not tie down
my body on purpose.

Clemency.
With my abdomen cut open
I wait for the serene coming
of nothingness.
The look that stops the flow of blood,
the lips that bury . . .

Time grows and prolongs the goodbyes.

The Scream is a Kind of Coffin

The clear form of your face
bears witness
to the clandestine passage
of time,
the one who wins the favor
of all endings.

The scream is a kind
of coffin.

Some sort of
mistake.

Some
catastrophe.

Or perhaps an
involuntary skill —
the truth that slinks in
naked
after an unexpected
storm.

Because in that flowing of essence
the unknown skin
may blossom.
The vertigo
where there is no reason,
where memory lives.

And to bear witness to its offering
the ignored forms
the profiles
that for awhile loved
then lost each other.

Events Like Palaces

Ridiculous dreamer:
pour your innocence
into the dark torrent that scares
you.

Build rafts
and separate your shadow
from yourself.

Don't let your diffuse
limits drown
in oracles.

Prefabricating
events
of imprecise axiom

like palaces —
a place to live astonished
in dreams

while reality
comes closer,
swimming toward your shore.

Things of the Blind

A face shines, anchored in fog:
season of rising suns.
A mask wields its powers
in the planet's coming and going.
At the risk of being crushed, it decides
to establish its own rhythm,
divine the sun,
cut off the head of the giant
who is used to frightening princesses.

Carefully, it extends the epiphany
toward the edge of instinct.
Shawl of solitude presupposing
the last traces of courage.
A promise sews up its nakedness,
crystal needle through lips.

Yesterday's grandmother brings sounds
like closets
where hope would have slept.

Her solitude imposes larks
that embroider
the innocence of clouds in the sky.

Go slowly over the stones
Don't let the green scream
of the enthusiasts scare you.

Don't believe to much
in your own fable.

It might be a good idea to calm down
and carefully measure the distance.

Because the space you will cross
is wide like time.

And we mice don't have wings.

Translated by Steven F. White.

Close to Me

· ·

Magali Alabaú

Magda Alabaú was born in Cienfuegos, Cuba, in 1945 and at ten years old travelled to the United States with her family. She has devoted herself to the theater and founded Medusa's Revenge, an acting company. She has published *Hermana* (1989) and *Hemos Llegado a Ilión*. Alabaú won the poetry prize given by the Association of Latin American Writers Living in the United States for *Hermana*.

. . . .

Sister

Let's go back to the rooms where we once walked
together
houses,
shadows,
night, mosquito netting,
buzzing. Also the dawn
and patios.
There were two patios, a big one where the chickens
the goats and the dog would meander,
there was the little green cemetery
where garlic was born
among two or three geranium bushes.
There was a window and we used to look out
a way to the patio.
Let's imagine a solitary
bus taking us back through all the rooms.
The living room
is first. They hide their faces when they see us come.
The armchair going around in circles. We sit down.
Imagining a carousel and dust.
We open the window and the other window
and then we shut them all.
The furniture is black.
The table has little embroidered mats.
We look at the dolls,
dancer, elephant
and giraffe and the three musketeer kings.
Our own beauty parlour there, the brushes,
the spray, cotton balls,
a carpet made of cut hair fallen to the floor, the mirrors, you and me.

Light bulbs above and I tell you
don't put on the light, the roaches are dancing,
discarded skates, two for the same foot.
The parlour keeps ghosts
who hide behind the sofa and the silent radio
says that it is late.

2.

I can't go on
because you are not here.
I come in. I open two or three letters
that speak of lost things.
The key gets stuck.
The door speaks softly. The dim light,
a little flame.
the bathroom, cigarettes,
no wine to remember the steps,
herb tea, bed.
I want to remember, but you disappear.
Night makes me remember
that I would have taken you
to a new country. As if illness
would run away through an airplane window.
You can bring back a memory, lull it to sleep
through the years, awaken it
in a poem, visit it
like you would a prisoner.
I'm afraid we have to dig deep
as if there were a treasure buried in the parlour
as if we had to write a short tale,
to make a little island in the patio
stretch the boughs and see ourselves as two plants
reaching up into the air.
The house has its boundaries.
It is an island. The kitchen belongs to grandmother,
the bathroom to all,
the dining room to grandfather
the living room to my mother
the two bedrooms are all ours
cutting us off from the rest.

We walk like fireflies,
twisted we stroll,
looking at hangers, starch,
mothballs.
We would have left the house in a minute.
The refrigerator would open,
the chairs would stack together on their own.
We would try to remember the lunches
but there is no wine, and memory
stays armored in a glass of water.

It's useless.
I don't have emotions,
soldiers ready to jump
I know that they all left when we came back
I know that they all closed the doors and threw something
like stones at us into the steets that were our living room.
But the street pushed us back in
and stuck out its tongue,
made faces, bared its teeth.
The furniture hid us and all around we knew
the war was about to start.
Planes in the park and sleepwalkers
shooting at the sidewalk,
let's throw ourselves down, behind the sofa.
I write my name with your tongue.
Let's knock on the floor to see if they'll open up.
Bullets fly by our heads.
The dolls are over there, let's drag them here
let them knock on the doors.
They peek out from the door. Yes, they wish
we had died in this battle.
We sit behind the sofa and fix our hair,
makeup our faces, put on flowers and
earplugs.
They look through the trunks, the radio, we aren't there.
Who are the invisible ones?

But we are lying down in my bed
twins, the same, telling our truths
in the cold, with no blanket
in front of a powerful eye

that looks at me insolently
while you say: It's over.
Now you have no body and I no soul,
in bed,
and I'll tell you that I was fleeing,
while I was filling more suitcases
and more excuses,
the more darkness was settling
on an island, a swamp,
a sorrow. Pulling out
our little story
and wanting a new page
to paint a zero there.
To extend oneself without ties,
without your eyes that see me a criminal.
And nevertheless I was the only one who understood
and this knowledge the only thing that would free you
and I ran away with it.

To be a deserter
means that any time
they speak of honor or fidelity,
love, heroics or other high things
you sneak away whenever you can.
It means staying out of conversations
and if you dare to put on a mask
you later take it off, relieved
no knowledgeable person was around.
It's not enjoying your meals, not sleeping like a log,
carrying your rope around in your pocket
and seeing, in case memory returns,
where to put the hanged man's noose.
It's being Peter, the cock and the three times,
it's knowing the sentences beforehand,
it's reading and not identifying with the hero.
It's rejecting the speeches and the awards,
and the small joys.
It's looking at the glass with your own teeth inside
and letting no one say why you cry.
Suddenly you have to take care of someone
to bathe a dog to help a blind man
cross the street and the word "lie" jumps out at you

unexpected and cold.
To be a deserter is to have left behind your eyes,
to prepare for suicide
and never carry it through.

Translated by Mary Jane Treacy.

Aida Cartagena de Portalatin

Aida Cartagena de Portalatin is one of the Dominican Republic's most distinguished poets, short story writers, novelists, essayists, and editors. A college professor, her most important collections include *Mi Mundo el Mar* and *Una Mejor murió sola.*

. . . .

Humble Litany

(One Voice)
For the word which burns like Joan at the stake
take not Your Word from us, O Lord.

For the word which flows under the skin
For the word which dries up the mouth
For the word which erases the lovely horizon
For the word which gives language to flesh
For the word which leans toward the brink
For the word which makes possible the exercise of love
For the word which speaks to thoughts
For this word and others, take not Your Word from us, O Lord.

For the word atom
For the word bomb
For the word missile
For the word war
For the word death
For this word and others, take not Your Word from us, O Lord.

For the word love
For the word sex
For the word birth
For the word child
For the word mother
For the word father
For the word brother
For the word friend
For this word and others, take not Your Word from us, O Lord.

For the word sacrificed in silence
until by his acts man sets it free

and it spills into other bodies
For the just word in the mouths of the just
For this word and others, take not Your Word from us, O Lord.

(Chorus)—
Two tribes take the earth.
Two tribes take the gold.
Twelve tribes are left without shelter
from the sun and the rain.
For the tribes without gold
without fields to grow wheat
For these and for others, take not Your Word from us, O Lord.

Second Elegy
(Fragment)

My mother was one of the great mothers
of the world.
From her womb were born seven children who would be
in Dallas, Memphis, or Birmingham
a racial question.
(Neither black nor white.)
Lala, who kept her house for thirty years
does not forget her and each time
the cold wind comes down our valley
those who were given her light, warm blankets
remember her too.
Mama knew nothing of political theory
(papal encyclicals or Karl Marx).
She only understood that the poor suffered hunger,
begged bread, needed shelter.
One lady journalist called her
a one-woman program for social assistance.
And now women of virtuous lives and those
who missed the straight path
miss her sorely.
Her acts were the duties of love.
Mama. Olimpia. Mama.
The public should not raise monuments
to sacks of groceries, blankets, roofs.
Such things are the duties of love.

Translated by Emma Jane Robinett.

Black Autumn

elegy
"Echoing drums, echoing on . . . "

I know it was already autumn,
without leaves and a lark's song.
I, who cry for the trees, for fish and doves,
reject the white men of the South,
those whites and their hatred aimed at black men.
I'd never question their motives
because they would answer
that in Alabama both races can blossom.
After the summer of Medgar W. Evers,
came the fall of four black girls.

The funeral procession of so many caskets.
That procession clouding happiness
the beaten drums, echoing on
Until when? Those four black bodies.
The light of their dark skin brightening the earth.
The time for joy has gone.
Afflicted, even the earth cries . . .
Even Death weeps for those four black girls.

Who can fill the empty place they leave? Brutally murdered.
Death owns death and no one else should dare to use it.
Their tender bones will lift up their race.
Their curly hair will knit flags.
Four were the girls murdered in the church,
four immortal torches sown in the South.
How can one spell F R E E D O M in Alabama?
I ask —
I who cry for trees, fish and doves.

Translated by Daisy Cocco De Filippis.

Gabriela Mistral

Gabriela Mistral, born in Montegrande, Chile in 1889, is a singular phenomenon in Latin American literature. Mistral won the Nobel Prize for Literature in 1945, the first Latin American to do so. The first comprehensive anthology in English, *A Gabriela Mistral Reader* (White Pine Press), appeared in 1993. Among her principle works are *Desolación* (1922), *Lecturas para mujeres* (1932) and *Poema de Chile* (1967).

. . . .

Rocking

The divine sea rocks its
       myriad waves.
Listening to the loving seas,
       I rock my child.

At night, the vagabond wind
       rocks the wheat.
Listening to the loving winds,
       I rock my child.

The heavenly Father silently rocks
       thousands of worlds.
Sensing his hand in the shadow,
       I rock my child.

Close to Me

Tender floss of my flesh
that I wove in my deep organs;
tender floss so easily chilled,
sleep, close to me!

The partridge dreams in clover,

listening to its heart beat.
Don't let my breathing disturb you,
sleep, close to me!

Tiny, trembling herb
surprised by life,
don't leap from my breast.
Sleep, close to me!

I who have lost everything,
now shudder with thoughts of sleep.
Don't slip from my arms —
sleep, close to me!

Dawn

I expand my heart so that
like a cascade of fire
the universe may enter.
The new day arrives and its coming
leaves me breathless.
I sing like a high-crowned grotto.
I sing my new day.

Because of the grace
I have lost and found,
I am humble;
without offering,
without receiving,
I am welcomed
until a night's Gorgon
turns away, defeated,
on the run.

Morning

She has returned, and she has returned.
Each morning the same and another.
Anticipated yesterday
and forever,
she must arrive this morning.

Empty-handed morning
that promised and cheated.
Behold another morning unfurl,
leap like the deer of the East,
awake, jubilant and new,
alive, brisk, and rich with work.

Brother, raise your head
from your chest
and receive her.
Make yourself worthy
of the one that leaps
and like a halcyon,
pushes off and rises,
a golden halcyon,
swooping down with songs.
Hallelujah, Hallelujah, Hallelujah!

Dusk

I feel my heart melt
like waxes in the sweetness:
an oil of langour,
not wine,
fills my veins.

And I feel my days passing,
silent and gentle as gazelle.

Night

Mountains vanish . . .
cattle wander
and are lost.
The sun returns to its forge:
everyone has fled.

Fields are being erased,
the granary has sunk,
and my cordillera depresses
its summit and living cry.

Animals stray, slanting
toward forgetfulness.
And the two of us also encircle
the night, my child.

My Mother

1.
My mother was very small
like mint or grass; she hardly cast a shadow
over things, hardly,
and the earth loved her
when it felt her lightness
and because she smiled upon it
in happiness and in pain.

Children loved her,
and the old ones, and the grass,
and the light that loves grace —
it searched for her and wooed her.

Because of her, perhaps this love

doesn't rise up: that which without
a whisper walks and slightly speaks:
the grassy horizon
and the spirit of water.

To whom am I telling this
in a foreign land?
In the mornings I speak this way
so that I might make her appear,
and along my interminable route,
I march on speaking to the Earth.

And a far off voice
comes singing and arrives;
I follow it like a lost soul
and wander without finding it.

Why was she taken so far away
so that I cannot reach her?
And if she always helped me,
why doesn't she respond, descend?

Who carries her form now
to go out to find her?
She walks so far away
that her sharp voice doesn't reach me.
I rush through my days
like someone who hears a call.
This night that is full of you,
given over only to you,
take it, although you are timeless,
feel it, hear it, reach it.
Nothing remains of this day's end
but hope and anxiety.

2.
Something comes from faraway,
something is present,
something comes forward;
without a body or a whisper it comes,
but the arrival never ends.
Although it truly comes,

why does it walk on and not reach me?

It is you who walks lightly,
with steps of caution.
Arrive, arrive, arrive, at last,
most faithful and most beloved.
What do you need where do you dwell?
Is it your river, your mountain?
Or am I the one, who without understanding
creates the delay?
The Earth and sea don't hold me
like your song;
the dawn and dying sunsets
do not conquer me.

I am alone with the night,
the Great Bear, the Balance,
believing that through this peace
your word can travel,
my breath breaking it,
my cry, driving it away.

Come, mother, come, arrive,
without knocking.
Accept the vision and sound
of this forgotten night
in which we remain orphans
without a destination, without a watchful eye.

It is suffering like jagged stones,
frost and the rough surf.
For the love of your daughter,
agree to listen to the owl and the waves,
but don't go back without
taking me home with you.

3.
So arrive, give me your face,
a word in the wind.
And if you don't take me away,
stay tonight. Don't go.
Although you will not answer me,

---

everything tonight is a word:
a face, the wind, the silence,
and the boiling Milky Way.

So . . . so . . . more still . . .
Stay, morning has not come,
and night has not closed.
Time grows thin,
the two to be equalled,
and quiet returns,
a slow passage to the homeland.

4.
It must be this, Mother speak,
eternity has arrived,
days end,
and it is a century of nothingness,
between life and death,
without desire, the darkness.
What is there then if not
delays, changes?

What was this? How did it happen?
How does it incessantly endure?
I don't want to demand;
I proceed understanding, frightened,
tearful and babbling
the words that you gave me,
said to me, which melt into one passionate:
Thank You.

Caribbean Sea

For A.E. Ribera Chevremont

Island of Puerto Rico,
island of palms,
light body, light,
like a saint
lightly resting
over the water,
from a thousand palm trees,
like the tallest,
from two thousand hills
comes a call.

Island, sunrise of my joy,
without a body's affliction,
you are a tremulous soul,
nursed by constellations
in the siesta of fire,
perforated by dialects,
and again in the innocent dawn.

Passionate island
of sugar cane and coffee:
word as sweet
as childhood,
blessed with song
like a Hosanna!
Songless siren
over the sea,
the sea's offense
in the surf:
rope of the waves,
bitter rope!

Save yourself
like the white fallow-deer,
and like the new llama
from Pachacamac,
and like the golden egg
in the nest,

and like Ifigenia
live in the flame.
May the archangels
of our race
save you:
Michael, the avenger;
Raphael, the foot soldier,
and Gabriel, our conductor
to the last hour.

Before my feet
and vision fail me,
before my skin becomes a fable,
before my knees
fly in the wind . . .

Philippine Independence Day

The Empty Walnut

I.

The rippled nut
that you play with,
fallen from the walnut tree,
did not bear witness to the Earth.

I found it in the pasture,
it didn't know who I was.
Cast off from the sky,
the visionless one was ignorant
of its plight.
With it in my possession,
I danced upon the green,

but it was deaf and did not hear
the horses running.

Don't disturb it.
A season of night lulls it to sleep.
When spring arrives,
you will split it open;
you will return it, unaware,
to God's world;
you will shout its name
and the name of the Earth.

II.

But he split it open
without waiting,
and saw the dust fall
from the hollow walnut:
his hand filled
with dark death,
and he sobbed and sobbed
the entire night.

III.

Let's bury it
under the grass
before spring comes.
Perhaps, in passing,
the God of life
will see it,
and with his hands touch
the Earth's dead one.

The Little Box From Olinalá

for Emma and Daniel Cossio

I.

My little box
from Olinalá is rosewood
and jacaranda.

When suddenly I
open it, it exudes
a Queen-of-Sheba
fragrance.

Oh tropical
whiff of cloves,
mahoghany
and coral!

I place it here,
I leave it there,
it comes and goes
through corridors.

It boils
from Grecian frets
like a homeland of
figwood, deer
and quail,

volcanoes
with great apertures
and the aerial Indian
like corn.

Like so,
they are painted,
like so, like so:
Indian fingers
or hummingbirds

and thus it is
made perfectly
by the Aztec hand,
the Quetzal hand.

II.

When night
is about to fall,
because it guards me
from evil,

I place it on a
small pillow
where others place
their treasures.

It causes me to have
beautiful dreams.
It makes me laugh
and weep . . .

Through my hands,
the sea passes,
twin sierras,
furrowed fields.

One sees the Anahuac
shining again,
the beast of Ajusco
about to leap,

and the route
that carries the sea
is going to reach
Quetzalcoatl.

It is my breath,
I am its feet;
it is knowledge,
I am delirium.

And we stop
like manna
where the road
is already abundant

where they shout
to us halala!
the ladies of Olinalá.

Translated by Maria Jacketti.

Alfonsina Storni

Alfonsina Storni (1892-1938), one of the most controversial and well-known figures in Argentinian literature, was also one of the most important feminists of Latin America. She is the author of numerous poetry collections and theatrical works. Among her most outstanding collections are *El dulce dano* (1918), *Irremediablement, Mundo de siete pozos,* and *Antologia poetica* (1961), which contains all of her major work. A selection of her work was published in English by White Pine Press in 1987.

. . . .

To Eros

Here's how it was: I caught you by the throat
at the seashore. While you took
the arrows from your quiver to wound me
and I spied your full-flower crown on the ground

I gutted your womb like a doll's
and examined its deceitful wheels
and found wound deep into its golden pulleys
a trap that said: sex.

Then, on the beach, I showed you (you now
a sorry rag doll) to the hound of your deeds,
the sun, before a frightened host of sirens.

Up the whitening rise was climbing
your godmother of wiles, Lady Moon,
and I threw you at the mouth of the waves.

Words to My Mother

Not great truths do I ask you;
you would not answer in kind. I only want
to know this: while I grew in you was the moon
witness, abroad by the dark yards in bloom?

And while I in your bosom of Latin fervors
listening slept, did a hoarse and sounding sea
settle your nights and did you watch the water
birds sink in the gold of the twilight?

For my soul is all fantastic and fly-about
and a feather-cloud of madness enfolds it
when the new moon climbs the bluing sky.

And if the sea unlocks its strong bouquet
my soul, lulled in a bright singing of sailors,
likes to watch the great undestined birds go by.

The Siren

Take away the whirlwind of hours
and the cobalt of the sky and the garments
of my September tree and the look
of the one who would open suns in my breast.

Snuff the roses of my face
and make dread the laugh in my lips
and meager the bread in my teeth, do this,
life, and deny me the bouquet of my verses.

But leave me the machine of blue
that looses its pulleys in the brow
and one live thought among the ruins;
I'll make it inspire like a siren on a field
of cripples and the broken clouds
will make for the sky by it, sails unfurled.

Camp Fire

The log —
then flame
in the winter
night

Hundred
red-tinted
human heads
in ring
around
the fire

From a mouth
(one or another)
broke
a line
of song

Another
entwined with it
unravelled
silken
words of
rhyme.

Precarious,
the moon
loomed
over the cenacle.

black sierra
skirted the world
in profie.

I was desiring
a hand.
Not yours:
God's.

To walk on
by his side
in the night
on the snow-covered
crags.

Encounter

I met up with him on a corner on Florida Street.
He was paler than ever, absent-minded as before.
For two long years he had owned my life . . .
I looked at him, unsurprised, toying with my gloves.

And a stupid, harebrained question from me
filled his vacant eyes with a quiet rebuff;
what I asked him in a flippant way was
"How come your teeth have gone yellow now?"

He stranded me there. I saw him hurry across
the street and with his dark sleeve
graze the white form of some wayward girl
who was walking along the way.

I followed his retreating hat for a
while . . . after that, he was a
speck of rust receding.
Then the thick crowd gulped him back down.

The World is Bitter

The world is bitter,
unripe,
stalled;
its forests
filled
with steel points.
Old tombs
climb to the surface;
the seawaters cradle
God-awful
houses.

The sun is bitter
over the world,
choked in the vapors
rising from
the
stalled
unripe place.

The moon is bitter
over the world;
green,
pallid;
on her damp
skates
she hunts specters.

The wind is bitter
over the world;
it huffs up clouds of dead insects,
ties its broken self
to towers,
knots up in
crepes of weeping;
weighs on the roofs.

Man is bitter
over the world,

balanced
on his legs . . .
At his back
the all,
stone desert;
before him,
all
a desert of suns
blind . . .

Translated by Mark McCaffrey.

Alaide Foppa

Born in 1932, Guatemalan author Alaide Foppa was kidnapped in her country in 1980 and disappeared. It is presumed that she was murdered by the Guatemalan government. Her work is varied as she was an essayist, professor at the University of Mexico and the author of five collections of poetry, none of which have yet been published in English. Her principle works include *Aunque es la noche* (1959), *Los dedos de mi mano* (1972) and *La sin ventura* (1975).

. . . .

Wound

Your life hurts me, son,
like a recently opened wound.
They think that you have detached yourself from me
simply because you were born.
The cord is invisible:
an arrow in my side,
a ripened fruit
that does not abandon the tree,
a tender branch
threatened.
You are weaker than my hand,
more delicate than my eyes,
smoother than my lips.
You made me so vulnerable
that I feel fear:
your life depends on
a gust of wind,
whoever touches you lightly
hurts you,
at your side,
in the tepid folds
of your bed, death sleeps.
And even though you are
more mine than my hand,
oh my most tender little branch,
perhaps I won't know how to defend you.

First Portrait of My Son

An eager breath
moves his still humid lips
of tepid and sweet whiteness.
Translucent skin reveals
the fine tissue of his veins
the down of a tender peach
covers his head,
and his delicate hand
seems made of wax.
Did my nostalgia perhaps
pour into his eyes
the dark blue of the seas?
Or will the hazelnut color
of my eyes
appear tomorrow
in his uncertain gaze?
Weak, slender, defenseless,
his homeliness moves us.
The imprecise form
changes more each day
along the dark road of
transmitted blood.

What is his life?
Long deep dreams
shattered by a sudden moan,
blind greed stretching out
toward the maternal breast
hurried beating
of an ignorant heart:
a tremor, a whimper, a sigh.

Nocturne

A mother's dream
forgets almost
nothing.
The shadow of a sigh
disturbs it,
the echo of a pale moan.
In the dream she doesn't know
if the child sleeps by her side
or if it rests, if it still rests
in the hidden bed
of its own life.
That sleep without rest
does not stop being a nest
while gentle breath
fills the night
without forgetfulness.

Your Hand in Mine

My hand is weak and delicate,
but if your hand looks for it,
it feels strong,
because your hand fits in it
exactly
and it nests in it with confidence.
Your hand is small
fleshy and warm,
and so lively that I
feel your whole impatient life
treading behind it.
You think that I hold you
and if I let go of you,
your hand waits

for me to capture it again,
as if it could not
remain detached
from my hand.
But it is your hand
that sustains my life.

Woman

Undulating grace
of distant adolescence:
like a hidden flame,
your whole desire stretches
toward an untouched
unprepared future.
Oh anxious creature
that no one stops,
now you even fear
the weight of a ring.

Love arrives,
and breaks your desire
the fear of ending
the hopeful weight:
love is a blind course
toward a single destiny
that impedes another track.
Captive creature
of your own hope
and your free desire.

There is no freedom.
Your tired gait,
suspended breathing
and your heavy belly

already taught you one day
that hope was
in buried blood.
Oh gentle creature,
fertility is
silent servitude.

That happiness
of childbirth, always
left you disconnected.
Hope so large
does not fit in you alone
and your grief grows
in a new land.
Divided creature,
you hide in your chest
an open pomegranate.

Little girl before the window
with the rose in your hand,
tender pregnant wife,
anxious sweetheart
or sleepless mother
who keeps on spinning her fabric
with hope and desires,
incomplete creature,
your life is barely
an insecure expectation.

Translated by Celeste Kostopulos-Cooperman.

Nancy Morejón

Nancy Morejón was born in Havana in 1944 and still resides there, working at the Fundación Pablo Milanés. Her books of poetry include *Mutismos* (1962), *Amor, ciudad atribuida* (1964), *Richard trajo su flauta y otros argumentos* (1967), *Piedra pulida* (1974), *Parajes de una época* (1979), *Octubre imprescindible* (1983), and *Cuaderno de Granada* (1984).

. . . .

Mother

My mother did not have a garden
but steep, cliffed islands
floating under the sun,
on delicate coral.
Not a free branch was there
on the orphan girl but many clubs.
What a time when, barefoot she would run
on the lime of orphanages
and she didn't know how to laugh
and she couldn't even look at the horizon.
She had neither an ivory hall
nor a wicker room
nor the silent vitraux of the tropics.
My mother had her song and her shawl
to rock the promise of my affections
and to raise her unheeded queen's head
to leave us her hands, like precious stones,
before the cold remains of the enemy

To a Boy

Between the foam and the tide
his back rose
when the evening was already
falling alone.

I had his black eyes, like herbs,
among the dark shells of the Pacific Ocean.

I felt his affectionate lips
like salt boiled in the sand.

Finally I felt his fragrant beard burning
like incense under the sun.

A wordly boy was upon me
and Bible songs
formed his legs, his ankles,
and the jewels of this maleness
and the wet hymns born out of his mouth
covered us, yes, like two navigators
tied to the uncertain sails of love.

I am alive in his arms,
and in his strong arms
I wanted to die
like a wounded bird.

Havana Harbor

Masons, cart drivers and occasional fishermen
　　　are walking in the sunlight
along Havana's shore
the blue and unaccustomed sea already covers the bare wall
little Gabriel squeezes a mango

　　　far away
a rum drinker kills himself
with a poised knife

　　　far away
a boat sets out to pierce
the center of the sky

there ruddy-faced men keep walking,
carrying black asphalt
　　　on their backs
while the sea remains unacccustomed and blue

I Never Saw Great Lakes

On this island where I was born
I never saw great lakes,
or small green lakes,
　　　　　or yellow ones,
or pure, clear lakes
in the center of the valley.

But when the hurricane roars
my clothes are torn
and a lump forms in my throat
and a pounding rises up to my head
and the sparrow's nest is
shaken, wet, empty . . .

Tree of Earthly Delights

To Sergio Moreno Carmenate

This is the tree of earthly delights
The painter declares
that this is the tree of earthly delights.
I want to name it.
Branches, leaves and fruits
will devour your eyes.
This is the tree of earthly delights
but its sap, like fire,
flows only when the painter
believes it should. That fire will light your view.
This is the tree of earthly delights.
I have come to name it
only when the painter decides
that this may be the tree of earthly delights.

A Tame and Ferocious Animal

They tell me I live on a cloud
and I agree
but it is not that simple anymore
the roosters also live there,
with as many words as tears
and, in the midst of turmoil,
with the spirit of the people
like a king of the atmosphere
rocked by the wind of the sky.

Requiem for the Left Hand

For Marta Valdés

All kinds of lines can be traced on a map,
        horizontal, straight, diagonal,
from the Greenwich Meridian to the Gulf of Mexico
            lines that more or less
reflect our idiosyncrasy

there are also very large maps
                in the imagination
and infinite terrestrial globes
        Marta

but today I guess that on a very
        small map
the smallest
drawn on notebook paper
        all of history can fit
everything

Poem Fifty

For the exterminating angel
of Sergio Moreno Carmenate

Jade water runs
by the house
It is any Tuesday
of a seventh week.

Angela Dominguez, Ever Present

You are somewhat slighter
you sing with troubadours and guitars
on the clearest night
as clear as your eyes

you seem to entangle yourself among golden pulses
and to recognize a ship of bamboo
in order to carry dreams in your arms
and breathe now for the peace of the tomb

you are the embodiment of laughter
                        Angela
here in my room
all these years you have been in a portrait
            and a dried, withered flower
            for the dead

You are the sweetheart of my dreams

Carpet

Without warning, the idea of the poem
enters through the window,
perhaps, with a scent.
By chance was it able to deceive so many misguided longings . . . ?
It is as if
someone would slip a carpet under my feet
and on solid ground, I might begin
a new flight, I as benevolent as
that reader whose dream cherished
Boti's reading . . .
I can't . . .
Oh unshaken dream
oh clear sails coming toward my red body . . .
And the idea of the poem
is no longer here,
is no longer here.

Will-o'-Wisp

Near a window,
during an evening of carnival
she watches the crowd
spilling drinks and smiles and foam.
She takes a deep breath
and unknowingly
from her eyes emerges
a tall will-o'-wisp.

Translated by Joy Renjilian-Burgy.

Fanny Carrión de Fierro

Fanny Carrión de Fierro (1939) received her doctorate in literature and linguistics from Pontificia Universidad Católica del Ecuador, Quito in 1981. She is curently a visiting professor at Willamette University in Oregon, teaching Spanish language and literature, and Latin American culture and civilization. Her publications include numerous articles, essays and literary studies published in journals, newspapers and magazines on subjects such as women's issues, human rights, children's rights, indigenous and grassroots movements, and linguistics. She has received numerous awards, among them The Gabriela Mistral National Poetry Award in Ecuador (1958, 1961, 1981 and 1985), and the National Poetry Award in Ecuador (1962).

. . . .

Heart of Time

And the sun was born
over the silence
of unconquerable space.

And love descended
like an angel
over the pure
and thundering stone.

And the priest spoke
above the brilliance
of the sleeping future.

Land of clean entrails,
bed of the universe,
Cañari oracle,
pyramid and mystery.

River of labyrinths
hidden and dark.

Mist that clears
for the prophecy

of favorable beginnings.

Stone of harsh fire
Ingapirca
womb
Cochasqui
the crossroads.

Impatient
bound-up mountain,
uncontrollable hope,
dawn,
maize and chahuarquero.

Dragon and macaw,
exorcism and serpent,
living pillar
of light and new tongues.

When the light falters
among the breeze
and brings you
words without meaning
visions you have never seen,

when the intruder
breaks the sun on his sword,
take care then
for your life and your seed,

return to the mountain
pass through the river
do not let your eyes
turn to forgetting.

But forgetting
rises up from the abyss
in the sleeping heart of time,

and stone upon stone
sorrow is shaping its triumph
for the final destruction of death.

Oracle

You who can see the future,
oracle,

tell me,

where playful words of joy,
and songs have their beginning,
where so much love and loneliness come from.

You who can see the future,
oracle,

unveil my sleeping forest,
my islands,
and my waterfalls,

and awaken the shrine
where my ritual lamp,
my blue beach
and my sunsets wait.

The Secret

Will you find out the secret,
you who know everything?

Think.

With this love
that I carry like a bird
hanging from my waist,

with this flowering

of moons and planets
and music and spheres,

with this crossroad
of pleasure and pain
which is born on my skin
and gives shape to your image,

why not speed along its flight,
hold back the wind
and faithlessness,

and why not change
bold, daily and ambiguous doubt
to certainty and joy,

what more to ask
of time and eyes.

If you find out the secret
you will be in love with love,
you,
who know everything.

Speak to Me

If I could only hear
about your mysteries,
your doubts
and your delusions,

the seven dawns your hand touched,
the seventeen deaths,
the six hundred faces,
the hundred thousand words,

Speak to me.

Open up your lights and darkness,
your silence and your song.

And tell me
there are feelings lying
in the depths of the volcano
and that emotion slumbers
as fiery and as naked
as the altar of the air
over the chasm.

Only You

If you have conquered
the glacier and the summit,
wiped out sadness,
reconstructed love
and destroyed weeping,

and if with the power of your eyes
you have bound up jaguars,
let loose doves,
opened up torrents,
drowned lakes and seas,
cast spells upon the past,
and defeated death,

then the ritual of your embrace
is true

and you are only you,
only you.

Grain of Sand

Do you see that hummingbird,
spark that ignites
the first ray of sun
in the morning?

Do you see that branch
that restlessly
opens its arms
to the mouth of the wind?

And do you see
how the bud trembles
when the cruel beak
breaks through its corolla
to pierce its most intimate secret?

Or the magical trace
that the sparrows leave
upon the grass
when they kindle their wings in flight?

Or how the warm bushes
alarmed and shy
shrink before being consumed
in the fierce conflagration of midday?

And have you seen
how water surrenders,
silent and gentle,
in the stubborn battle of the rocks?

Or have you heard how
tree and breeze,
jaguar and dove,
sing their song,
dance their dance,
cry out their loneliness,
and shatter their fears
at the brink of the chasm?

All that is only
a moment's grain of sand
crumbling beside the sea
compared to the lightest touch
of your voice and my voice
or your love and my love.

If Time Waits

If time waits
roses will return,

> and again
> there will be fire in the twilight
> restlessness in the air
> and passion in the light,

> and again
> sounds will play in our hands
> and desire in our voice.

If time returns
silence will fall quiet,

> and again
> grief will burn
> its last banners
> and sensual happiness
> will sound its songs.

If time is quiet
death will die,

> and again

our skins will glow
and pleasure will cry out
in all our senses,

and in the round moon
of our embrace
love will let loose
its burning bird.

If time dies

I will be I again
and you will be you.

Hidden Pleasure

Hidden pleasure
of waiting for waiting,

consolation of silence,
hint of a caress,
outline of shyness
and excesses,
absence of absence.

Evening will flutter
its trembling flame in the corners,
and the light of this sun
with no shadows at noon
will sing in our words.
You will reach out your hands

toward old delusions,

I will touch the fresh rain
of your open gaze.

And it will be the end
of every ending
and the beginning
of every beginning.

Oblivion

Yes, oblivion will come
at the boundary of time.

Now,
strip bare your mysteries
and your obsessions
in the silence,

lean your question
between my doubts
and cradle this passion
ancient and blind
next to the evening and its wonder.

Will the moment return
with its portion of love?

Who knows?

Who will tell
the fortune of the evening stars
if we will no longer be ourselves?
And who will interpret

the tarot cards to death?

Neither you nor I.

And memories
will turn dust to dust.

Ah,
who knows,
perhaps without suspecting it,
you and I
always will be you and I
at the boundary of time.

Translated by Sally Cheney Bell.

María Arrillaga

María Arrillaga is a Puerto Rican poet and has been a professor at the University of Puerto Rico at Rio Piedras. She is also the secretary of PEN's women's committee. Author of numerous collections of poetry, Ms. Arrillaga is currently living in New York City where she is working on an autobiographical novel.

. . . .

Dream

The granddaughter was a guerrilla.

The grandmother was a gadabout.

The daughter wanted to rest.

The granddaughter tenaciously struggled to build a meaningful life for herself and for everyone else.

The grandmother was terribly afraid she would be left alone.

The daughter wanted more than anything else to create.

The granddaughter had left everything behind her in order to find herself. Only her life mattered. Live your life. Don't live mine, she said.

The grandmother knew who she was only in terms of personal and family relations.

The daughter felt trapped. The granddaughter had abandoned her. The grandmother screamed for attention.

The grandmother was very angry and rebellious.

The daughter was afraid that they would not let her live.

The grandaughter had disappeared and nobody knew where she was.

The granddaughter was very angry and rebellious. She felt lonely and abandoned by the daughter and the grandmother. She left in order to become a guerrilla. She joined a tribe of women who believed in freedom for all human beings. They staged ritual choruses where they rhythmically named those valiant, loving, generous women who had courageously managed to realize themselves to the point of being anywhere securely centered and aware of a growing tradition of strength. They knew no fear, coercion or isolation. They trusted their ability to do whatver needed to be done at any given moment. And to be, simply to be, because of the community of affection, generosity and valor they shared. The granddaughter had entered a different dimension from which all women could be happy.

The daughter created when she was able. The demands of the

grandmother were always there and the granddaughter had disappeared. One day she received a letter from the granddaughter. Dear daughter, it said, we need your experience. Please share it with us. The daughter answered.:

Dear granddaughter:

It is good to be courageous, loving and generous. To suffer no fear, coercion or isolation. I feel alone because you have left me and grandmother's demands make me afraid.

Tbe granddaughter replied:

Dear daughter:

I am a mirror of yourself. I belong to your tribe.

The daughter understood that she would never want for anything and went to see the grandmother. The grandmother was out gadding about. The daughter returned home and went happily to sleep.

Mariana II

Motherhood is so final, Nita,
I muse, feeling to the point of hurting
my absolute love for you.
The attacks you hurl at me set us free
and I bear up like the ancient cathedrals.
"They also serve who only stand and wait," said Milton.
I wait for you, my lovely child, as your beauty blooms
opening up to so many things in Apollinean splendor.
Today I watch your sad and pretty face telling me that you
are beginning to understand.
I leave you and I love you more than heaven.
My father left me and he loved me.
My mother deserted me in anger and fear.
Your father abandoned me and I loved him.
But I leave you so that we both may live.
So that I may be my own person. So that you might also be.
So that I might at some moment entice time into letting me write
my finest poem for you.

Like Raquel

I have discovered that I'm like Raquel,
like my aunt Iris,
like my grandmother Irene,
like María Luisa,
perhaps a bit like mama,
sometimes, in my voice
and when I put my fist
under my left cheek
When I was very young I didn't much like
these women in my family.
I grew up and liked men a lot.
I grew up a bit more
and now I have discovered
that I'm like Raquel
like my aunt Iris
like my grandmother Irene
like María Luisa
perhaps a bit like mama
sometimes in my voice
and when I put my fist
under my left cheek.
Let me explain,
that of these five women
two are old maids
and the other three
had serious marital problems.

Rosa/Filí

I.

His skin like cream is free of wrinkles
It is the classical background for distinct features
His countenance is placid
As an anomalous day at Isla Vede
He shaves and does not irritate
His skin is cool as cool as he
The man is a model of calmness
His voice intelligent and tranquil
Attests to his self-assurance
He quietly cares for you and his three children
While you and the children love him with ardor.

II.

Your skin, Filí, has furrows
That conspire against your placid visage
Your features are blurred
Sometimes twisted in baroque strokes
Like daily bread cosmetics no longer irritate
You get irritated by how much, at last, they weigh
Often your irritation becomes stridency
That conspires to conceal your intelligence
You are not calm, Filí, nor safely self-assured
To have and keep his love you must become alpine
And even reach tempestuous heights
What you must do to keep his tranquil love, to keep their love,
Is far too excessive.
(Father is ardor
Mother is peace)
Even so, someday he might leave
With someone with creamy skin
A voice calm and sweet
A placid face framing distinct features
But you will keep what you already know, Filí
That's no small thing
And, who knows,

Perhaps he'll stay with you
(Why abandon such bliss?)

III.

He did not leave
You left, Rosa, Rosario, Rosiña, Rosaura/Filí
Your name grows
In that new path
Furrows flee your face
Your features are refined
In the contour of precise strokes
Calm you are
The towering heights of the past
Become the happy landscape
Of your big waist
Your hair undulates defying
He who will not appreciate your body
You are intelligent, Filí
You have your life
You have yourself
It's no small thing.

Silence That Can Be Heard

Amanda Berenguer

Uruguayan Amanda Berenguer (1942) is known for her experimental and avant garde poetry. She is an important literary figure in her country. Among her works are *La invitacion* (1967) and *Materia prema* (1972).

. . . .

The Signs on the Table

> be[for]e my tortured brothers and sisters

what metaphor could possibly convey
              the headless slaughtered thunderclap of
pain
and lay the signs on the table?

i say searing raw rosettes
     rings of red-hot coals
     cupfuls of rekindled clotting
and i choke
as i hear her nipples crackle
that woman bound by marauders
          to her deathstone

then i say breathing primitive wheezing
         snorts of another species
         aftermath of wounds
and that ravished mangled vagina
the vital membranes exposed set ajar
and i break my neck
      my voice cracks
      on the threshold of each violation

i hear a cry suddenly aborted
      blocking the exits
    a shapeless last sound expelled from the body
while entrails bleed torn
      and impaled
and my speech comes unhinged

what metaphor can possibly send ships
            to rescue mournful news?

The testicles robust defenseless seedbeds
writhe beneath the sparks from the electrodes
and extracted fingernails grow
                        still joined by the ropes we call nerves
to the rumble of broken bones
                while the skeleton is flogged or stretched
— the frame that endures their doggedness —
and i hear that acoustic almost impersonal witness
                    gushing from deep inside the marrow
breath — true to the end —
            gathers up the pain (that secret roar)
and hurls it at the deaf dirty walls

the word where is
                the right one
for aspirated vomit
for sewer water in their lungs
black immersion in the ebb and flow of oxygen
full of rot and excrement?

or the word for that body astride
                                the iron sawhorse
that horseman riding a knife between his legs
and for that savage thread
the howl that binds his entrails to the air?

a parched throat is no source of words

now the scene is stripped bare
                a face with empty eyesockets
only mute images surround me
                vocal cords missing

falling vanquished i stammer:

someone/ there is a face/
dripping/ decapitated birds/ weeping tears/ weeping
blood/ mother/ oh mother lick my entrails/ drape my
heart in deep blackness/ now the flutter of wings/ the death rattle
the shadow covering the fire/ now the look in those eyes/ mother/
my eyes shatter/ words

on detailed engravings i had watched the bodies staked under the
sun on lithographs or wrapped in fresh hides so the coils of the wind
would crush them

i saw spoonfuls of molten lead thrown into their mouths amid sym-
metrical stones outlined in ink and i watched while tongs penned
with deep clean strokes tore out well-drawn pieces of tongue on dis-
play cases at the castle of the Counts of Flanders

i saw the wooden rack with toothed wheels they showed Galileo one
ominous night in Rome (that device would stretch the arms and legs
slowly without haste until tendons snapped along with joints like tree
trunks like dried fruit like anatomical drawings)

then there was young Pope Urban VIII who gave orders to kill all the
birds in the Vatican garden because their songs annoyed him

i was observing the details of the flames like golden lizards like
bluish-red flowering branches that consumed Joan of Arc while
twelve servants hold the Chinese Emperor's nightingale by twelve
silken strings

and i watched the four subtly drawn black horses dismember the
bodies of Indians by dragging them in all four directions in the plazas
of my South America

i had seen pictures
travelled the globe
read the texts

but i invented blindfolds

                                        scratched out images
                                        scratched out access roads
           at times i realized and denied it

           i realize now
                         it's happening so close by
           within the walls of this city
           within these walls
                                   the well of suffering boils over
                                   right now
                                   it's boiling over
       the morning is sweet
                       a sun-drenched blue cake
                       shared by children
       a woman in radiant yellow
                              gets on the bus
       the green of the traffic light forecasts favorable winds
       on a nearby street
                       right now
                       this very minute
       in a dingy spot with no exit the well of suffering boils over

       routine domestic savagery
                              hangs like a bladder edged with needles
                              or a black hornet's nest sweating stingers
                              or an infected porcupine of gooey glass

       a machine thick with straight hair
                       resembling a rat
       drags a living creature by the wings
       pounced premeditatedly
       more than a bulldog more than the red-necked vulture
       on the stalked probed beaten prey
               torn apart dragged along by a rope
               at his throat at the very place
       whence the signs might come and the names
                       that no one will confess
       sequestered cast into shadows with no day or night
       when the hands point to a single question: who am i?
       the horse with broken teeth and jaw
       sinking his hooves into quicksand
       the horse's gaze approached the judge's bench

outstripping the vulture in his flight
outstripping the skinny-flanked dogs
lines threads of his gaze crossed the triangles
the projection of infamy
and there arose in him an untapped power
the spirit of a bud sprouting amid the frost

the torturer is afraid shudders
flings himself on his prey
to wind up a fearsome exercise in discipline
and the horse is dealt furious gusts of domination

pain puts on its spurs
                              and on orders from the higher ups
it's time to seek an answer
                        a forced abortive answer
and the cables pull from inside his lungs
and the horse resists the horse holds out dripping blood
no longer a horse no longer a person

who dares put into words the length
of that thread of life
                        burning slime
oozing from his eyesockets uncontained?

it isn't death no
                        it isn't death
it's more than death
        it's the cutting blade swift and still
        the clamor of teeth set on edge
        the frenzy of nerve
it's the tender raw flesh
    a faint throbbing at the quick
the spot probed openly
        where pain resides and is rekindled

they wield electric whips
        rigid fiery blows
                        and they rouse him

thorax belly head limbs mark the boundaries
of a minutely precise roman circus
where the fierceness of pain devours memory
and eternity is measured in swallowed chunks of self

"this one has had it"
"throw him off the dock he's food for the fish"

the inquisitor with his lamp
                        nothingness howling through its broken chimney
upholds a tainted justice convulsed
                        like a woman addicted to drugs

but it sometimes happens that the body is more than bait
its surrendered hiding place as well
        like an asset attached

the body draws back from itself
        glimpses salvation
        glimpses a vague moon that blinds it
and abandons its mangled self
                        in a corner of its being

at once slippery urine changing shift
        eggs with green clots inside
        rattles full of pumice stone
        off-schedule rattles
                        hooded

watchful right inside the cage
        recurrent hornets
take down the thick-haired spider
repair the web of molten glass

near the severed ear a lifeline bobs
abandoned bits of flesh surface still palpitating
"in the cradle of hunger"
                there emerge
"teenage jasmine flowers" "with five teeth"
"with five orange blossoms"
                   over the shipwreck
"with five tiny
ferocities"
        and they sink
there's a sound of liquid red passion flowers draining
                through a hole of cartilage
rutting gears fill with sand
           and chunks of liver
the minutes wallow among scorpions
that suction the ever dark navel
and there's a fall
        and a wait as for a death sentence
hands flailing in the void

the word tumbles from its scaffolding as well
        is drawn and quartered
remains an invalid in the midst of all that happened

neither the vertiginous womb
nor the entire imagination unfurled
could possibly conceive
           another's suffering
           someone else's pain

each body bears its own witness:
a glory flower that blooms but once
           each night

in childbirth as in earthquakes
pain was central to the backbone of the world
but it was a tulip standing tall
        a vital volcano
        a memorable flowering

pain has no memory
there remain only half-buried teeth
        gags
        sleepless objects
scraps of metal sunken in an obsessive bloody mire
that rises slowly
        or grows all at once
from deep in the chest
        so fiery
that it melts thick boughs of solid fear
encrusted in the resistant ribs

and leaves movable scars
        internal
        in darkness
        scurrying to and fro
fleetfooted centipedes in a flooded cellar

i swallow saliva
words betray me

i acknowledge receipt of your letter Dostoyevsky
"i bow down to all human suffering"
and lie prostrate
        before the door of the prison cell
        before my tortured brothers and sisters

Translated by Louise B. Popkin.

Carmen Naranjo

Carmen Naranjo (1930) is one of the most interesting cultural figures of Costa Rica. She was ambassador to Israel in the 1970s and served as the Cultural Minister and the author of the system of social security in her country. Naranjo is most well-known as a novelist. Among her works are *Canción de la Ternura* (1964) and *My Guerilla* (1966).

. . . .

Part One: The Orders Begin

III

Over the crying comes the sugar, the cooing,
the refreshing pat and the stroll:
all is new, budding life,
opening eyes to the astonishment
without knowing more wonder
than to sharpen the pupils and to sigh.
It is good and also sweet
to not forsake the cradle
and to rock in each step
because the surprise of the child
has the mark of innocence.
The cry comes and over the cry
a stretching that goes
from deaths to resurrections
in scenes that we memorize in penumbras
because the mystery of the hidden places disappears.
The train that runs and runs does not stop
in the stations of the fair,
happy passengers do not enter, no one sings,
someone cries ants with elephant legs,
another sickens and vomits,
the noise of furious bees,
and the train does not stop when it smells bad,
when the atmosphere is dense with words
that stun with dizzy falls.
My station, very far, shows the dawn,
and to her comes a chorus of canaries in gold cages,
they trill free hymns of very old times,

made by groups of new slaves
in lands of water, sun and generous harvests,
because to live is to acquire endless play
and the channel is the path that one travels
to end at the altar of the absurd.
An image sticks to the window,
its eyes among the trees that run and run,
the lips over the neighing of the rails
say things I do not understand.
The dreams catch fire in the passing lights
and the image is lost in a curve
or when going through a tunnel with the cold of cemeteries.

Perhaps it was God that appeared to count the passengers
and to decide if some should go by another way
or if many must remain in the instant
or if they, the family that flees, arrived at the place
or if that place is mine and there I will trap the solitude
so that it will be solitude of high borders.
In the immobility of the window
I discover the tattoo of my wounds.
Weak to the point of not hating, scarcely loving,
clever in the neglect of skills,
wise in the construction of spider webs,
nomad over the dream camps,
merchant of stars and ant hills,
immobile witness in the center of decadence,
strange habitant of the convulsion of the centuries
          and of this century,
innkeeper of friends, each one in their room, with their key,
useless collector of all that is useless,
able to cloister oneself and then break the doors
because life passes and death comes,
because the noise is a coiled ball that explodes,
because history is a book half read,
because someone paints a portrait in the middle of night,
because the face of God is hard,
because the river is a sculptor of stones,
because I did not always want to live,
because I did not always dare to die,
because at times the road is short,
because at times the road is long.

The train becomes a street and the street a mystery of shop windows
with the odor of chemical formulas in retorts:
one definition seems to be the key
and is very easy to write a woven phrase:
I am a weave of fears and cowardices,
the rest is hidden.
With the sign in the plaza, as in the final judgment,
to wait for the caprice of the scales,
punished with pointed stones, pummeled,
fire in the feet, sores in the nails,
or perhaps a flower, an applause,
the plaza is able to give solidarity of nudes
and at the end, who cares,
one has suffered, always
and genesis an enterprise of imperfections.

IV

First I looked for the faith and then the destiny.
Perhaps destiny was the faith
or faith the breakage of destiny.
Who knows? The bird flies,
the horse rides, the man screams
and the scream is faith in destiny
in the destiny of no faith.

Translated by Shaun T. Griffin and Emma Sepúlveda-Pulvirenti.

Emma Sepúlveda-Pulvirenti

Emma Sepúlveda Pulvirenti (1950) was born in Argentina and moved to Santiago, Chile, at the age of seven. She had nearly completed a B.A. in Latin American history at the Universidad de Chile when Allende was overthrown in 1973. She fled Chile in fear of persecution and later completed her studies in the United States. Eventually she received her Ph.D. in twentieth century Spanish poetry from the University of California, Davis. She is an associate professor of Spanish at the University of Nevada, Reno. An accomplished photographer, many of her photographs have been published in books or on covers of books by South American female poets. Currently she is working on an anthology of Chilean poets. Among her recent books are *Los Límites del Lenguaje: Un Acercamiento a la Poética del Silencio* [Critical Essays] (*The Limits of the Language: An Approach to the Poetry of Silence*), 1990; and *Tiempo Cómplice del Tiempo* [Poems] (*Time is the Accomplice of Time*), 1989.

. . . .

September 11, 1973

Santiago, Chile

We shall overcome!
I heard at eight
we shall overcome!
I heard again
at nine

and at ten
and at eleven
and all
the hours
in the petrified day

after

the voices

lowered

weakened

folded

and the silence

devoured the echo

echo
       echo
echo
       echo
echo
       echo

without me realizing
it became
the sound
of bullets
against the body
of those who rose in opposition.

No

No,
no
not
numbers.
They are not numbers.

They are names.

To the Child that Never Was

One day I dreamt myself
the maker of lives
and I seized
the womb
the sinister smoke
that invents our children
I imagined your eyes
would become mouths
that would never cease to demand
the right to the fertile corner
of all the mothers
I do not know why
I asked with a cry
the right to shape you
from a weak clot
from a mass of nothing
for you to create yourself
human like the others
the sons or the daughters
that are grown in the
uterine linings
in the test tubes
of the laboratory
or in the beds of silk
that thirst for bodies
I gave myself the exclusive right
to draw you in my thoughts
and in the intimate, sickly
cavity of a sleeping
womb
that split you in pieces
of dead blood
when you innocently
wanted to be flesh
of my own
miserable flesh.

From Now Until Chile

there are long kilometers
of anguished exiles
that pursue me when alone
I want to return again
to sleep in your arms
with the brush of a kiss
on the eyes
and the vow
to begin to deny
the next disappearance.

Translated by Shaun T. Griffin and Emma Sepúlveda-Pulvirenti.

Gioconda Belli

Gioconda Belli was born in Managua, Nicaragua. Her poetry collection *Línea de fuego (Line of Fire)* received the Casa de las Américas Prize. Her novel *La mujer habitada (The Inhabited Woman)* won the Prize for the Best Literary Work of the Year from the Union of German Publishers and Editors. Her work in English includes *From Eve's Rib* (poetry) and *The Inhabited Woman,* both published by Curbstone Press.

. . . .

The Blood of Others

I read the poems of the dead.
I survived.
I lived to laugh and cry
and I shouted *Patria Libre o Morir*
from the back of a truck
the day we reached Managua.

I read the poems of the dead,
watching the ants on the grass,
my bare feet,
your straight hair,
your back arched at the meeting.

I read the poems of the dead.
Does the blood in our bodies that lets us love each other
belong to us?

Birth

I remember
when my daughter was born.
I was all aches and fear
waiting to see
emerging through my open legs
a nine-month-old dream
with a face and a sex.

Nicaragua Water Fire

Rain
Window view of water on leaves
wind passes swishing skirts
muddy waters uproot tree trunks
trees paint stars puddles of blood
borders of a day that must be fought
there's no other way no alternative but the struggle
Behind curtains of water
I write fingers on triggers
great wars
suffering the size of mothers' eyes
dripping uncontainable cloudbursts
here come the small cold corpses
los muchachos come down from the mountains
with hammocks they recovered from the contras
we don't eat much there isn't much we all want to eat
big white hands want to kill us
but we made hospital beds
where women scream births
all day we beat like hearts
tum tum tam tam
Indians' veins repeat history:
We don't want children who will be slaves
flowers blossom from coffins
no one dies in Nicaragua
Nicaragua my love my raped child
getting up straightening her skirt
walking behind the murderer following him
down the mountain up the mountain
they will not pass say the birds
they will not pass say the couples who make love
who make children who make bread who make trenches
who make uniforms who write letters for the mobilized troops
Nicaragua my love my Black girl Miskito Sumo Rama
Maypole dance in Pearl Lagoon
hurricane winds blowing down the San Juan River
they will not pass and it rains on the young soldiers
tracking the scent of the beasts
never letting them rest following them pursuing them

uprooting them from the motherland's breast ripping them
       out like weeds
never letting them strike
we want corn rice beans
seeds taking root in the land
where a *campesino* keeps his Land Reform title in a wooden box
don't let the devils pass to announce the coming salvation
to the people who saw farms burn
and a neighbor murdered in front of his wife and children
Nicaragua my child
she dances she's learned to read to talk with people
to tell them her story to get on planes to tell her story
to travel around the world telling her story to everyone
speaking tirelessly in newspapers written in
       incomprehensible languages
screaming getting angry furious
all the noise she makes seems incredible so does the way she resists
planes mines speedboats bombs curses in English
speeches on how to bow one's head
and she fights breaks free flees
and there goes General Sandino and the hill the rocket launchers
the green columns advancing clearing land
building sugar mills
rivers of milk houses schools
young men telling their story
limping from the hospital
taking a bus to return to the north
wind that shakes fear
we were born for this
we rejoice for this
rage and hope clenched between our teeth
no rest for us no rest for them day or night
tiny but stubborn country
Nicaragua fearless spear daring wild mare
pastures in Chontales where Nadine
dreams of Percheron horses
and we have a fountain of dreams
we have a factory of dreams
a dream assembly line for the unbelievers
here no one gets away without a scratched conscience
no one comes here without being moved
country of enlightened lunatics poets painters

showers of lights schools dance
international conferences protocol
school-age police sweetly scolding
flesh and blood of people who sometimes are right
        sometimes make mistakes
who try and try again
everything moves here a dancing woman's hips
singing out a lust for life against the mummies
speaking of death hoping to earn their return trips
on printed pages that come out in the afternoon with their lies
and their rage of frustrated hysteria
envy of the girl who sways as she walks
winks sells tamales sells nail polish
joins the militia goes to the park invents love
sets the flowers of the *malinche* tree on fire hides to bewilder
comes out marching amidst drawn bayonets
sets up the circus and fairs and prays
and believes in life and death
and prepares swords of fire
so that the only choice can be
earthly paradise
or ashes
patria libre
or *morir*.

Brief Lessons in Eroticism I

I.

To sail the entire length of a body
Is to circle the world
To navigate the rose of the winds without a compass
Islands gulfs peninsulas breakwaters against crashing waves
It's not easy — though pleasurable —
Don't think you can do it in a day or night of flowing bedsheets
There are enough secrets in the pores to fill many moons

II.

The body like an astral chart has its coded language
When you find a star perhaps you'll have to begin
Change course when a hurricane or a piercing scream
Makes you tremble:
a hollow in the hand you didn't suspect

III.

Pass a certain curve many times
Find the lake of the water lilies
Caress the center with your stay
Submerge drown stretch
Don't deny yourself the smell the salt the sugar
The intense winds shaping cumulus nimbus within the lungs
clouding the brain
Tremor of legs
Numbing tidal wave of kisses

IV.

Steep yourself in the humus slowly
There is no hurry, no wearing out
Don't try to reach the peak
Delay the threshold of paradise

Cradle your fallen angel
Tousle her silky mane
brandishing your stolen sword of fire
Bite the apple

V.

Breathe
Ache
Exchange glances saliva impregnate yourself
Turn entangle the skin that slips away
Find the foot at the end of the leg
Search for the secret step
The shape of the heel
The crescent bay of the arch
that forms the footprints
Savor them.

VI.

Listen to the shell of the ear
How the dampness moans
Earlobe approaching the lip sound of breathing
Pores that rise into tiny mountains
Shivery currents unsettling the skin
Descend gently the bridge of the neck to the sea in the chest
Whisper into the sound of the heart
Find the water's source

VII.

Traverse the Land of Fire
The Cape of Good Hope
Navigate mindlessly the joining of the oceans
Sail over the algae arm yourself with coral howl wail
Emerge with the olive branch cry bring forth all hidden
tenderness
Disrobe the looks of wonderment
Hurl the sextant from the heights of the eyelashes
Flare the nostrils

VIII.

Inhale sigh
Die a little
Sweetly slowly die
Agonize within the gaze sustain the pleasure
Turn the rudder spread the sails
Sail on turn towards Venus
morning star
— the sea like a vast mercurial crystal —
Sleep you shipwrecked sailor!

Translated by Steven F. White.

Ana María Rodas

Ana María Rodas (1937) is a poet, journalist, and literary critic from Guatemala. She has published four poetry collections, *Poemas de la Izquierda Erótica, Cuatro Esquinas del Juego de una Muñeca, El Fin de los Mitos y los Sueños,* and *La Insurrección de Mariana,* which won the 1993 Central American prize for poetry, as did *Mariana en la Tigrera* in fiction. She is a professor at the University of San Carlos.

. . . .

Poems from the Erotic Left

I came, doctor, because my head hurts.
There are nights when I don't sleep
start to suffocate, and feel restless.
Besides, at times I'm depressed.

Of course I took my pink capsules
in a somewhat irregular way, it's true.

The tongue? Clean.
Thirty-three, breathe deep.
Pressure normal, good reflexes.

And in the midst of the farce
of the cold stethoscope, tranquilizers,
telling me how it's going
and regards to the family
shamelessly, they lie with impunity.

What a pity they don't put men up in jars yet
        like ampules
        like little capsules
        like pomades.

This doesn't make it, they say.
It's not poetry because I talk about contraptions.
                    The kitchen.
About what it costs,
when there's no desire
to work.

I write simply what I feel.
Everything is poetry, since for me
a drop of rain is worth the same
as black smoke.

They interrupt me: You're right!
Rain is a poetic subject,
but diesel exhaust, that's a municipal problem.

Yesterday's shadows
the inexhaustible stones of a river far away,
consciousness is but memory
of the dead
who kept on doing their work.

                    Things dead that kill,
long lean bodies
(I always liked tall men)
sleep now
                    lower your voices
let me live today the dead memory of tomorrow.

                    Will we ever really live
or will we only be dreaming
an eternal dream with the slight odor of semen and water?

Everything is nothing more than one
interminable black hole at the end
of which   comes another
black sack of silence. One small
death
awaits each day.
The calendar tacked to the wall
marks time
and my skin, my hair, thinner by the moment
would mark, if they could,
the smooth movement of the sea where
I would be a perfect corpse.

Time is bringing out in me
qualities I seek daily:
next to my meager
          the sea's lushness
love that rolls in on itself
and two or three persistent friends who do not give up
regardless of my countless faults.

It's made of plants, absurd tricks
by light bulbs that light up
turn off
or burn out.
A lot of time is spent turning my back
on the rules made by men.

You are doing fab, great leader.
I am the guerrilla under your regime
                    the ob   ject
who rises up in arms   of love
between your arsenal of guerrilla egoism
                    and the power you imagine
at the end of your long march.

Track well my footprints
                    on your soul
and without scruples crush
any bud of subversive tenderness
before love takes hold
and your tidy dictatorship
                                        turns to shit.

I know
I'm not going to be anything more than
a guerrilla of love.
          I'm situated somewhere
in the erotic left.
Shooting bullet after bullet
against the system.
Wasting strength and time
preaching a corny gospel.

I'm going to end up like that other wacko
                                the one caught
at the end of his rope in the sierras.

But since my struggle
is not political nor of use to men
they'll never publish my diary
nor produce for popular consumption
posters
and pins with my portrait.

Revolutionary: tonight
I won't be in your bed.
Don't be surprised at love's subversion
                              old master.
You are so cocky, so correct
and yes, very worried about social problems.
Two-faced you overlook
that in your house
you fit to a T
those role models from the best of tyrants.

I adore you
you are
my people.

But in your hand there's an automatic weapon
and in your eyes, dark police.
                    There is no
communication between my love
            and your   violence.

Translated by Zoë Anglesey.

Teresa Calderón

Teresa Calderón was born in La Serena, Chile in 1955 and studied Latin American literature in the University of Chile. She is considered to be one of the most outstanding poets of her generation. She published *Causa Perdida* in 1984 and has been awarded numerous prizes, among them the Fundacioñ Neruda Prize for Poetry.

. . . .

Affairs of Memory

What country is it that I see,
what names descend
along the walls of the old houses?

Where is the hand
that chased away the giant of the long dream?
What became of the magical vine
and where has Puss and Boots
gone?

What rambling shore sometimes returns
disinterring glimmers from memory?

What happened to the little stork
what became
of its games
and its comings and goings through time?

Only a laugh persists:
a fairy hunting butterflies
while erasing from the map,
with only one plumed stroke
all the paths to return.

Exile

And tomorrow:
what will become of the faces I invented
to search for me,
and of the words that I could not imagine
in my presence?

Tomorrow, I ask
what will become of the land of the weeping araucaria
and of the anonymous bird that ate from the plum trees
beyond the cement and wire fences?

Tomorrow,
what will become of the shelter among the linden trees,
and of those who waited so long for a return?

What will become of the little boy that we left
protected among the violets
and who still winks like a secret
between us?

And tomorrow
what will become of the rain that cooled down
the apple trees
in the corner of our eyes?

Will life perhaps be an infinite twilight
and the street an immense motionless mirror?

State of Seige

Considering the graveness
of the most recent events,
and the internal disorder
that is being lived in my country these days.
Considering also the continuous subversion of my sentiments
and the successive
insurrection
of my will,
I request reinforcements
from the Highest State of my conscience.

It emits an edict that
immediately establishes
the emergency situation,
and to protect the citizenry
it lines up a robust army
of defense mechanisms
with strict orders
to give up one's life if necessary.

My anarchic heart
accepts a provisional government,
while I continue
in clandestine negotiations with your eyes,
with your mouth invading all my limits,
in this war that you pronounce to me
in this open love between us.

Domestic Battles

I began losing the battles.

Accordingly, I ended up losing you.

With a shadow radar
I pursue you among so many people.

There you are scrunched up in your trench
with an escort of accumulated hatred
unravelling kisses in a useless sheet.

With me you sustain the most savage struggle
because it is the last of all.

From now on I will be the guerilla fighter
the one who takes your mouth by storm
the one who installs her flag in your memory,

the one who dies of love in other arms
believing that she is invading
the distant territory of your body.

"From Your Depths and Kneeling . . ."

There is a little glass boy
arrested in time
or shipwrecked.

His face is in all the mirrors.

His face repeats itself in each face.

He is hidden
in a family secret.

Translated by Celeste Kostopulos-Cooperman.

Belkis Cuza Malé

Belkis Cuza Malé was born in the region of Oriente in Cuba in 1942. She later moved to Havana where she worked as a journalist. In the 1970s she came to live in the United States where she worked as editor of *Linden Lane* magazine. Among her books are *Los Alucinados, Tiempo del sol, Cartas a Ana Frank, El Clavel y La Rosa* and *Women on the Front Lines* (Unicorn Press).

. . . .

Glance

Look, look at yourself in the mirror.
Those curling lips,
those dark circles, those eyes
give you away.
If you really wanted to,
you could unwrinkle your brow
and paint your mouth.
Like this, with no make-up,
go on across the street,
go sit by the reefs
and watch the years go by,
the parade of soldiers marching by,
and the tanks, and the wagons,
and hearses.

Greek Metamorphosis

Sappho was neither woman nor man.

In the midst of a Greek city's fauna and flora,
        men busy with men,
Sappho sketched a *salty sea*, a ship

a barrel of fresh water.
She made herself go from port to port
with her servant girl to round up the slaves,
dark-skinned boys
eager to make their sex felt.
Of one she made a darling little girl
who kept her busy the rest of her life.

No one knows how she died; getting along in years,
she closed her home to the curious.
History tells us she wrapped her face
in a silk shawl, pronounced
a couple of jumbled sentences,
and changed to a butterfly
        that still lives, still flutters
around the lamp
or above Proust's hat.

And Here are the Poets in Their Sad Portraits

And here are the poets in their sad portraits,
quill in hand — peacock blue or dried India ink.
There's still a logical gleam in their eyes;
a delicate hand props up the head the executioner severed.
In the fashion of the time, they compress their fervor
into the thin thread of their mouths.
Believers or nonbelievers, stoics or rebels,
they always proclaim the future,
always stand on the highest rock,
hear the ocean creaking but never head off its fury,
sip rum in taverns
and love from turbulent lips.
But most terrifying is what they write,

words no one dares put into his own mouth.

And here are the poets in their sad portraits.
Meditative or merely choleric.
Fuzzy faced kids from small towns,
family men,
fussy old codgers,
women both tender and troublesome.
Some are grown fat on bad living and bad food,

but they are clever and they outlive their judges.
Some have given up the beard and mustache
for a cynical smile.
Behind their backs, we speculate
about the world and these poets.
Tenderness is made official in their name.

And here are the poets in their sad portraits.
A window or sunny park is all they own.
In the background, curtains are drawn;
over their death beds, a screech owl watches.
Robert Browning (for example)
had beautiful eyes.
And who remembers the face of Hopkins?

The young speak elegantly about Rimbaud.
Dante symbolizes terror.
And Byron loved his mirror.

And here are the poets in their sad portraits.
Now their faces hang in galleries,
illustrate magazines.
Doesn't that silence tell you anything?

Women Don't Die on the Front Lines

Women don't die on the front lines,
their heads don't roll like golf balls,
they don't sleep under a rain forest of gunpowder,
they don't leave the sky in ruins.
No snow freezes their hearts.
Women don't die on the front lines,
they don't drive the devil out of Jerusalem,
they don't blow up aqueducts or railroads,
they don't master the arts of war
or of peace, either.
They don't make generals
or unknown soldiers carved out of stone
in town squares.
Women don't die on the front lines.
They are statues of salt in the Louvre,
mothers like Phaedra,
lovers of Henry the Eighth,
Mata Haris,
Eva Perons,
queens counselled by Prime Ministers,
nursemaids, cooks, washerwomen,
romantic poets.
Women don't make history,
but at nine months they push it out of their bellies
then sleep for twenty-four hours
like a soldier on leave from the front.

Poet's Biography

For the poet's biography,
forget the tone of voice he spoke in,
his wartime loves,
facial features,
(brown eyes, hapless nose),
family life,
the way he made enemies,
his amazement, laziness, talents.
Forget who brought him into the world,
what month and what year it happened.
You have only to deal with
the cities where he didn't make love,
the kind of woman he desired,
the ways he was influenced by Blake.

For the Moment

For the moment, we've run out of starry nights,
and love birds in moonlight.
The hard summer did it all in,
dried up the lawn
and wiped out every trace.
A small street lamp lights up the scene.
I know well this summer was hard and long.

Creed

If it's true you made light
and shadow.
If your voice is inaudible
and your sight eternal
like yourself,
tell me, for God's sake, what I'm doing here,
one small woman,
waiting for heaven or hell?
Please forget all about me
for better or worse.
Better to live in a painter's mind
　　　　　　　to be dreamed.
That, only that,
or be a fallen branch in a forest.

Translated by Pamela Carmell.

Chiqui Vicioso

Chiqui Vicioso (1948) returned to the Dominican Republic, her homeland, in 1980 after having lived in New York City for eighteen years. There she published her first book, *Viaje desde el agua* (1981), a collection of poems which established her as one of the poetic voices of the Dominican Republic. Her poetry is known for its honesty in confronting issues and giving a voice to the voiceless.

. . . .

Survival I

Look for the address
write it out
look for a stamp
toss the letter in the mailbox.

Water the plants (today is Monday)
write to Mayra (it's a year and a half since I've done it)
organize the slides (the rest are waiting)
write the article about Guinea-Bissau.

Call Nani and María Margarita
and I don't have the details for the conference
call Rayner, set up the date.

and now it's twelve-fifteen.

TWELVE-FIFTEEN

. . . tomorrow will be Tuesday.

Survival II

Tomorrow will be Tuesday
the photos will be ready
I must judge,
choose, classify
then have the copies made
and then wait.

Then I must send letters
with photos for Augusta
and I will have defeated death
for the coming hours
minutes and seconds
and perhaps until next week.

Perspectives

One looks around and sees
Eudocia hard-working and convinced
that for herself, Reginaldo and their children
Alfonso and Rita there is no way back.

One looks around and discovers
Rosa with her faith in the lottery
"these dreams are better than the movies,
they cost one dollar and last a whole week."
One watches Maria Luisa sighing over
the soap operas that uplift her,
one hears her repeat as an excuse:
"in this loneliness they are my happiness."

One watches the working women in the subway
hiding their mistreated hands,
untended nails, hiding behind glasss

the circles under the eyes, dark, permanent.

One watches blue collar workers
during rush hour gradually deafened by
a noise similar to, as the *Daily News* has stated,
the sound made by a jet's landing.

One watches the young latinos
"loose joints," "acid" and "loose cigarettes"
boys of few years who lost
their original humanity on these streets.

And one watches the girls too,
an adolescence brief, fragile, going:
stripped of illusion at twenty,
brought to childbed by Mondays and diapers.

One looks at the garbage, the trash
on 103rd street, at the drunks;
at the people hunting for "specials"
in the second-hand clothing stores.

And one begins to feel differently
this bad air; to walk over the dead
fighting against death itself
to try to make a new life.

Fazal

Fazal
all eyes on the clock
marking twelve o'clock the rhythm of the kitchen
at last the rose in the midst of the rain
at last the sun of Karachi in his hair
at last the Melody of his voice
ordering a sandwich
at last his love
of tomatoes and lettuce
his kisses of cheese
cucumber and ham
at last her eyes on his hands
when he cracks hard boiled eggs
eyes filled with dark tears

Melody will think that it's because of the onion.

Translated by Emma Jane Robinett.

Wo/men

Wo/men draped in black
multicolor socks and strong arms
hair and moustaches, hairy legs
hormones and hairs . . . patchy with suffering.
Sad women, who never smile
lacking teeth, lacking dreams
women/ earth, dirt farm and hoes
women/ cabbage, tomatoes and wool
women/ man, child and tenderness
iron women, rock women.

Haiti

I imagine you a virgin
before forerunning pirates
had removed your mahogany dress
to leave you thus
with your bare, round breasts
and your torn grass-skirt
barely green,
timidly brown.

Haiti,
I imagine you an adolescent
fragrant vertivert, tender with dew
without the numerous scars
displayed in the traffickers' maps
and multicolor banners sold
on the sidewalks of Port-au-Prince,
Jaimel, St. Mark, and Artibonite
in a dramatic tin plate bargain.

Haiti,
traveller who eagerly smiles at me
interrupting the quiet of paths,
softening stones, paving dust
with your sweaty, bare feet
Haiti who can give art a thousand shapes
and who paints the stars with your hands
I found out that love and hate
share your name.

Translated by Daisy Cocco De Filippis.

Marjorie Agosín

Marjorie Agosín (1955), a native of Chile, is a professor of Spanish Literature at Wellesley College. She is the author of numerous books of poetry, criticism and fiction. She is also the editor of White Pine Press' *Secret Weavers Series*. Her most recent work is her first book of short stories, *Happiness* (White Pine Press, 1993).

. . . .

When she showed me her photograph
she said,
This is my daughter.
She still hasn't come home.
She hasn't come home in ten years.
But this is her photograph.
Isn't it true that she is very pretty?
She is a philosophy student
and here she is when she was
fourteen years old
and had her first
communion,
starched, sacred.
This is my daughter.
She is so pretty.
I talk to her every day.
She no longer comes home late, and this is why I reproach her
much less.
But I love her so much.
This is my daughter.
Every night I say goodbye to her.
I kiss her
and it's hard for me not to cry
even though I know she will not come
home late
because as you know, she has not come
home for years.
I love this photo very much.
I look at it every day.
It seems that only yesterday
she was a little feathered angel in my arms

and here she looks like a young lady,
a philosophy student,
another disappeared.
But isn't it true that she is so pretty,
that she has an angel's face,
that it seems as if she were still alive?

Memorial

Memory, like a piece of beautiful and imprecise canvas
accumulating the embers of wrath,
the beauties of an expansive tenderness that is
stretched
to the very base of a sword of faith which expands
to become a table where
everyone writes what he wants
or does not want to remember:
a blade of smooth wood where we can invent
maps of our most cherished possessions,
memory flying opposite the sky,
dark and luminous,
folded and always
transforming itself
into a necklace of words
strung between the captive stones
that cannot say anything.

Translated by Celeste Kostopulos-Cooperman.

The Most Unbelievable Part

The most unbelievable part,
they were people like us
good manners
well-educated and refined.
Versed in abstract sciences,
always took a box for the symphony
made regular trips to the dentist
attended very nice prep schools
some played golf . . .

Yes, people like you, like me
family men
grandfathers
uncles and godfathers.

But they went crazy
delighted in burning
children and books
played at decorating cemeteries
bought furniture made of broken bones
dined on tender ears and testicles.

Thought they were invincible
meticulous in their duties
and spoke of torture
in the language of surgeons and butchers.

They assassinated the young of my country
and of yours.
now nobody could believe in Alice through the looking glass
now nobody could stroll along the avenues
without terror bursting through their bones

And the most unbelievable part
they were people
like you
like me
yes, nice people
just like us.

Disappeared Woman V

I had no witnesses
to my death.
Nobody carried out rituals, wrote epitaphs.
Nobody came near
for a veiled
farewell.

No one could come
to my burial
because the silence of uncertainty
covered a body disappeared, dis-encountered
rising up treacherous amid the mists.

The authorities
have concealed me.
I do not appear among the morgue's murmuring bones,
I don't exist in the Cardex files
nobody saw me transmuted leaving my country.
Nobody put numbers on the soles of my feet.

I am a stray,
a hand fleeing and accursed.
I am made of rain and grenades
and when they call my name
I will appear
because I never went to my
own funeral.

Seven Stones

Today I picked up
seven stones
resembling birds and orphans
in the dead sand.
I looked at them
as if they were offerings
of uncomon times,
as if they were
seven endangered travelers.

Like a sorceress, I came near
and very gently
moistened them
against my cheek.

I wanted
to be seven stones
inside my skin,
to be, for an instant, very round and smooth
so somebody would pick me up
and make clefts in my sides
with the damp voice of the wind.

I wanted
you to pick me up,
to kiss me,
so I could be a river stone
in your estuary mouth.

I keep the seven stones
in my pocket.
They make a mound
in my hand
and in my stories
of absences,
a mossy sound.

Language

Your tongue like a barefoot walk
along the coasts of mine, your tongue
approaching the threshold of my mouth
is a silky blade of grass, a caress so sweet
it clings. Your tongue defying prohibited
back rooms of the lips,
moving back and forth
over the body luminous with love.
Your tongue
creating meadows over the face, sailing,
shiplike, over the breast reposing beside you
like a water plant.
Your tongue, the image of my tongue,
becomes for a moment
moss,
water,
stone.

Translated by Cola Franzen.

Claribel Alegría

Claribel Alegría was born in Estelí, Nicaragua in 1924. She grew up in El Salvador where she was educated in Santa Ana before attending George Washington University. Author of more than fifteen books, some of them in collaboration with her husband, Alegría has written novels, short stories, and children's stories, as well as poems. She has also edited numerous anthologies and is a widely published translator.

. . . .

Accounting

In the sixty-eight years
I have lived
there are a few electrical instants:
the happiness of my feet
skipping puddles
six hours in Macchu Pichu
the ten minutes necessary
to lose my virginity
the buzzing of the telephone
while awaiting the death of my mother
the hoarse voice
announcing the death
of Monsignor Romero
fifteen minutes in Delft
the first wail of my daughter
I don't know how many years
dreaming of my people's liberation
certain immortal deaths
the eyes of that starving child
your eyes bathing me with love
one forget-me-not afternoon
and in this sultry hour
the urge to mould myself
into a verse
a shout
a fleck of foam.

Ars Poetica

I,
poet by trade,
condemned so many times
to be a crow,
would never change places
with the Venus de Milo:
while she reigns in the Louvre
and dies of boredom
and collects dust
I discover the sun
each morning
and amid valleys
volcanoes
and debris of war
I catch sight of the promised land.

Erosion

I don't want to see you
no
I have another face
now
that one
the one you loved
remains forever
in your pupils.

Nocturnal Visits

I think of our anonymous boys
of our burnt-out heroes
the amputated
the cripples
those who lost both legs
both eyes
the stammering teenagers.
At night I listen to their phantoms
shouting in my ear
shaking me out of lethargy
issuing me commands
I think of their tattered lives
of their feverish hands
reaching out to seize ours.
It's not that they're begging
they're demanding
they've earned the right to order us
to break up our sleep
to come awake
to shake off once and for all
this lassitude.

Silence

An explosion your death
and then this silence.
After the silence
what?

The Grandmother

Time stood still
that afternoon
when the husband,
her second,
took a hammer and smashed
the gold watch,
a gift from the first,
the deceased.
The watch she always wore
pinned to her bosom.
As if you were someone else you watched him
throw the pieces into the fire
and said nothing.
Seated in your rocking chair
you coined endless rancor
rocked your hatreds
your loves
rocked past the death of the abductor
and fell silent.
The children moved you to the attic
and there in solitude,
lips pressed tight
you kept on rocking.
You listened to your chair
creaking against the wooden boards,
tried to reconstruct the tick-tock of the clock.
The rhythm wasn't the same
the hours no longer flowed by as before
the same eternal day
the same light filtered through the glass
the same day
installed forever
in your attic.
Life and death the same
in your eternal purgatory
"*triqui triqui triqui tran
los maderos de San Juan
piden queso y les dan hueso
piden pan y no les dan*"

and the people down below
don't want to listen
they think it's Sunday
because visitors have come
and there is roast chicken
but it's the same day
the same everlasting day
you speed up the rhythm
they've stopped talking
and you rock faster
faster
triqui triqui
triqui triqui
triqui triqui
triquitran
the door shatters
and I hurtle into your arms.

Have Pity

Have pity on our brother
who has lost his wonder
and finds everything
just as it should be
and never defies
the forbidden.
Have pity because he is dead
and there's nothing we can do
but send him flowers
and bury him as soon as possible.

Translated by Darwin Flakoll.

Letter to an Exile

My dear Odysseus:
I simply cannot let
another day go by
without writing you
about my life here in Ithaca.
It's been many years
since you left.
Your absence was painful
for your son
and me.
I soon was besieged
by suitors
they were so many,
so persistent their advances
that a god, taking pity
on my anguish
advised me to weave
a silken cloth
never-ending
that might serve
as your shroud.
If I finished it
I would have at once
to choose a husband.
Quite taken with the idea
each day at sunrise
I began to weave
unravelling each night.
Thus did I spend three years
but now, Odysseus,
my heart longs for a younger man
as handsome as you in your youth:
as skillful with bow
and spear.
Our house is a shambles
and I need a master
who can take it in hand.
Telemachus is but a child
and your father an old man.

It's better, Odysseus,
if you don't come back
men are weak;
they can't take rejection.
Of my love for you
not a spark remains.
Telemachus is just fine
he never even asks about his father
it's better for you
if we think you're dead.
I've heard from travellers
about Calypso
and Circe.
This is your chance, Odysseus
if you choose Calypso
you'll regain your youth
if Circe is your chosen
you can be chief
among her swine.
I hope this letter
doesn't offend you.
If you invoke the gods
it will be in vain
just remember Menelaus
and Helen,
on account of that crazy war
our finest men
have lost their lives
and you are where you are.
Don't come back, Odysseus,
I beg you.
                    Your discreet Penelope

Translated by Louise B. Popkin.

Belinda Zubicueta Carmona

Born to working-class parents in Santiago, Chile, in 1955, Belinda Zubicueta Carmona was detained by the repressive military apparatus of the Pinochet regime and was only recently released fom the prison of Santo Domingo. She was the only woman political prioner held in Chile. She has contributed to many anthologies including *Poesía prisonera* (Prison Poetry), *Ante la vida* (Before LIfe), and *Girasoles en la sombra* (Sunflowers in the Shadows). She published her first book of poems, *En una costilla del tiempo* (On the Border of Time) in 1990. The poems included here are from *Ardiendo Piedras* (Burning Stones).

. . . .

Stretched Out in Solitude

Unfolding moments
I gather your figure
    and stretched out
with my teeth pulling at the pillow
I make live
    reclining on
        the Andean range.

Storing Memories

The memories
    of my legs
retain your
    hand's caress
and
the moistened cloth
rests under the sheet.

Another Day

Along the side
      of the wall
on the aged footpath
Spring passs
and does not touch me.

Tenderness

Even though I'm angry
and gnawed between the teeth
your punishment will be
to see me smile
because you didn't remove
my tenderness
which you battered
      with the electric prod.

Daily Task

I pass a
        door
two padlocks
three locks
four keys
        I am finally
in a corner of the patio
and in the tender sunlight
I open a book of beginnings.

Smiling in syllables
        I scale a pause
          an instant
          a memory
I raise my eyelids
        in a daily task
          the sky grows large
in a surge of landscapes
        I incarnate a flower
          a leaf
            in
        my hands
        and a valley
        in my
              sex.

Between the Lines

Between the lines
I keep typing stubborness
about a bird
in restless flight.

I spin beneath a bronze sky
and filling the hem of my dress
with a swarm of bees and pollen
        I continue inhabiting
the smile of your dark moon.

While
a handful of slender leaves
tries to cross
        my cell.

Translated by Celeste Kostopulos-Cooperman.

The Moon's Cadaver

Clara Silva

Very little is known about Clara Silva (Uruguay, 1908-1976). This notable poet and narrator's work has not, until now, been published in English. By means of her poetry, Silva explores the dicotomy that exists in relationships as well as the existential anguish of being a woman. Among her works, *Los delirios* (1959), *La cabellera oscura* (1973), *Juicio final* and *Memoria de la nada* stand out. She is considered to be one of the first surrealist poets of Latin America.

. . . .

The Moon's Cadaver

The earth is hard enough
for your footsteps
the clue to your shadow
not the cemetery of clouds
where you look for the moon's cadaver
or the basement where you hide
forgotten causes
between the dissonant chords of memory.

Don't lose your space among men
beneath their open umbrellas.
Each hour
daylight disturbs the secrecy of its mice
for the cat that lies in wait.

Tea at the Magdalene

Where do I sit
to write my name
where do I place its syllables
furrrowed by the winds of danger?
Lost
among the ruins of disaster
— tea at the Magdalene —
the news satisfies me
like hungry mice
climbing through the bed
to sense that day is approaching.

Then
I let the newspapers drop
and read
in the obscurity of my conscience
the overlooked guilt
the sterile fig tree
transformed in the blind mirrors of time.

And placed between two provisional worlds.

Magical Devices

She had in her favor
the aura of anguish
the oracle of hair
and all the words
and vials used
in the medication of neurosis.

And so many other things
that deafened
when her own face became imperceptible.
But now
that she has "touché l'automne des idées"
she walks between her cantos
warriors of her tongue
burned by fever
in the furor of hope.

From so much filling and rising
and taking upon herself
the powers of hell
innocent creature of her history
She breaks the blood lock.

And can now recognize how useless
all the magical devices were.

Who Will Throw the First Stone?

The New Testament
droops
when you read it
comfortably installed in bed.
A deaf supplication
to the curse that runs
through the streets.
You are alone and guilty
for those dead souls who wake the earth.
You are dead and saved
in the city that constructs its history
among the clamour
and the obscurity of its cries.

It is impossible to sail between two waters
and to be your own shadow.
But who will throw the first stone
and call into question the man
who is tormented
between his crossings?

In the Darkness of the Other

They carried a shadow in the soul's place
and slept with it
vanquished by the earth
their mouths were like greedy sparks
in the descending path.

In the distance
and the pride
of engendering themselves
in the darkness of the other
they devoured
the terror of mortal beings
on the nuptial table.

Disillusioned
by the strange offering
that made them quickly
commune with the blood
they related the adventure of their lives
for each daybreak
of their fallen
bodies.

Translated by Celeste Kostopulos-Cooperman.

Giannina Braschi

Giannina Braschi was born in San Juan, Puerto Rico in 1954. She left the island at the age of eighteen and studied in numerous countries including Spain, England, France and Italy. She has a doctorate from SUNY at Stony Brook (1980). Braschi has taught at Rutgers University and at City University of New York and has written several works of literary criticism. Her books of poetry include *Asalto al tiempo*, 1981 (Assault on Time), *La comedia profana*, 1985 (Profane Comedy), and *El imperio de los sueños*, 1988, which was translated by Tess O'Dwyer and published as *Empire of Dreams* by Yale University Press in 1994.. She has also published a book of criticism, *La poesía de Bécquer: el tiempo de los objetos o el espacio de la luz*, 1982.

. . . .

I have been a fortune-teller. Ages ago, I told the fortune of buffoons and madmen. You remember. I had a small voice like a grain of sand and enormous hands. Madmen walked over my hands. I told them the truth. I could never lie to them. And now I am sorry. Ages ago, a drunkard filled with dreams asked me to dance. I used my cards to tell his fortune when his drinks became blows. My banging on the door killed the sea. Memories finished us. Madmen and buffoons count the grains of sand and have never destroyed night's dreams. They draw up the night and rise filled with middays. Magicians were and always will be my companions. Without guessing their tricks I started fire in their throats. But none explode. Maybe one. And with the fish another chimera rises.

I am the shepherd of hope. I am the dancing doll. I am the singer of the wind. I'll fly, I'll jump, I'll blow my golden trumpet. I am contained in the feet, in the head of the sea, in the eyes of the wind. And I feel I'm going to fall at the exact moment when rivers contract. I invite you to dance for me, to laugh at me, to say yes to me. I am your dancer, your maiden, your sewing frame. I am the act and the word. I have nothing. I am act and word. I have nothing.

A letter comes and visits me. Puts its legs up in the living room. Wanders about speechless. Suddenly it explodes and another shape appears. Welcome! It flees swiftly and I see two, three, four, five, seven, five-hundred letters. Suddenly I hear the word *river* and water runs in another river's space. I repeat *river* two, three, four, five, seven, five-hundred times, and cold imprisons twilight. Then this letter's twin slope trembles. There is no return without reaching bottom. The letter is born of life. That's where its limit began. I discover the world underneath.

Letters are not letters because they dream. There is something that barely marks each one, like a person's hands. These letters are not signs of another sign. The letter's rhythmic beat, when counting syllables, is life spelling its memories. And we stop at letters, hiding in the darkness of their syllables. And we say, I've lived five years in this letter. Here I forged a first syllable and a last silence. I forged enigmas and secrets too. From my letter, the way was born. And from my letter, the beginning and the current of other letters attached their syllables to the name. And I tell myself that each letter is an old memory and a silence.

No lagoon is darker or clearer or more full of mountains or planes than the first letter of your name. I said that I was made entirely of letters, and I used to say that the horizon would turn clouds into other signs, revealing other letters. But I didn't say that behind all those letters the horizon cuts the edge of my hand.

Ask. I don't ask for much. I only ask you for two numbers, two people, two accounts, two ways, two mirrors, two words, two gazes, two digits that always add up to four on a mirror, that always add up to eight and answer us, count. There's only two of us, you and I together. Ask. I don't ask for much. But for what little I ask the mirror repeats: only two are left.

Translated by Tess O'Dwyer.

Final Manuscript

. . .
That's when I saw fall a whole series of things
That I didn't understand. That I didn't know existed
That's when I ended up as if dead.
And I was still alive.

I stroke the ocean. I navigate. I stroke the night. And the bat.
I stroke the ocean. The low clouds of night.
The cobwebs. The memories.
All is fortuitous.
All is gratuitous.
Even the name. And its surname.
Even time. And its memory.
Even the beginnings.
The century.
The dark nights of the soul.
The bed where
hope
and its memory
lie inscribed.
All is fortuitous. I repeat.

It's necessary for everything to stop
for an instant
before it ends. Before the descent
and its beginning.

It's not this. I repeat.
The fall. And spring. And summer. And winter.
The same sky and
its stars fall.
I'm sick of so much of the same.
And I repeat it.

Even now I repeat it.
I fell into the tomb.
I fell into life.
I fell into death.
I hushed up all the memories.
I fell into night
and stayed awake.

They shimmer
and are made, as always, out of nothingness.
They are made and seem to be.
They wander by the same ocean.
By all the streets and avenues
God's little worm
and all its ominous hope
in a destiny which is suddenly crafted
like the shadow of dust and nothingness.

Like the same shadow
I was the cradle of dust
and of shadow
I was nothing
I was what I am
I was shadow of other shadows
I was dust of other dusts
I was shadow and dust and nothing.

Translated by Alan West.

Jeannette Miller

Jeannette Miller was born in Santo Domingo, Dominican Republic in 1944. Considered one of the most distinguished Dominican poets of the twentieth century, she has published four books of poems: *El Viaje* (1967), *Fórmulas para Combatir el Miedo* (1972), *Estadías* (1985) and *Fichas de Identidad* (1985). She has received critical acclaim for her work and is a tenured professor at la Universidad Autónoma de Santo Domingo and at the National School of Fine Arts.

. . . .

These Green Paths . . .

They were green paths in the placid time of the needle,
the pupil chooses its sole aim
in the peace of orange trees and cliffs.
We rented time,
and the song of the land in the placid moment of the shadows
resembling the rumor of the beasts
when they are free to roam between the undergrowth.
It was the time of friendship,
pain had taken us to peace
and our sweetness was sad like the smell of fruit
when night approaches.
In the mornings of the stone,
when the salt hits our senses with its silence
and a sensation of life engulfs us,
huge unknown villages would entrust us with their thoughts.
Rooms of light in a world of long manes,
the squeak of the sun embracing the sea, the stone,
independently.
Benign hospitality,
time of clean water, of lost stream,
between guanabanas and limoncillos,
mint,
round seasoned mangoes,
sweet nísperos . . .
Sometimes, like from another planet, the ocean fragrances
would approach.
Then the ocean was ours,
we possessed one another . . .

The Rise of the Afternoon is a Wide Glory

The rise of the afternoon is a wide glory
Reflections of light on the white walls.
The trees without constraint start dying.
Innumerable knives hang from their treetops.
There is no blood.
Only silence
Bridges of light dilute with me in an hour appropriate for the last death.
Surfaces of sun extend their silence.
I inhale your senses that fly through plains.
I,
finding myself in the radiance and the artists'
solitary amplitude,
memories . . .
because even on a Monday I need the word,
not a scream
only a bridge,
better a flight . . .
Mountains,
sky,
sea,
strange birds,
a slow sustainment,
death that returns the eternal cycles,
mutation,
word,
I,
symbiosis,
pollen,
galaxy,
time,
flower . . .
I will open a door.
I will open all doors . . .

This sense of space . . .

This sense of space, mine, familiar . . .
In the clarity of the pigeons, the simple people of always.
Tolling of the bells,
some droplets of water accompanying . . .
I wish never again to stir.

The Crazed Woman

She
wakes up each day with the dawn.
Dozes in the sun
saves the moments of silence for the solitude.
Leaning on an imaginary door she sees life
the patient life that she does not get to live.
She travels through the streets behind the voice which leads her
she surprises those around her with absurd complaints
she fills her fateful circle in search of excuses.
Lacking everything.
Reduced in her anxiety,
she receives night in retreat/ withdrawal
dirtied by a battering life
in her breast a furious animal.

The Woman I Know

The Woman I know
wields invisible fingers
scattered voice
curls and straightened hair
glass beads of luck.
Full of contradictions and fears
she knows herself scorned.
Covered by smoke and martyrdom
projected over decayed foundations
arched by the fire of man
reduced to rabid lava, impotent
demands detonating new life
words to alter the monotony
that will invent her a memory.
The woman I know
has a facial expression
which I would not want even in death.

Four times during the night

Four times during the night your eyes like white butterflies,
reluctant.
The moan of air inside your white time.
Man that enriches the sweet fall pasture,
we are late to this confrontation of shadows and prophecies.
My head, upright, next to the murals
of the world.
My head blind and solitary
in your burning madness.

I remember the long corridors . . .

I remember the long corridors where the shadow was continuous,
the everliving,
the scent of candles and flowers from the vaults.
I remember features of ever-present bird.
In a small room of animal sounds
the dry air of bougainvillea.
Narrow walls,
so great was the happiness of silence,
listening to time while we sat to live.
Clear skies, swallows,
the candles like a blow of prophesy.
Tall eyes,
the glow of the cloud blinded us,
our bodies grew eating the soil, the trees, the sound . . .
We were everything.

Bird dressed as solitude and tears . .

Bird dressed as solitude and tears,
I see your body elapse.
After the flows
After the bitter tears,
the song of the leopard in your eyes of wind.

Translated by Paula Vega.

Coral Bracho

Coral Bracho, born in Mexico in 1951, is considered to be one of the most interesting and innovative Mexican poets. Her first book, *Peces de Piel Fugaz*, was published in 1977, and in 1981 she published *El Ser Que Va a Morir*. Her most recent collection is *Bajo el destello líquido* (1990).

. . . .

From Their Eyes Adorned With Vitreous Sands

From the breath of these marble fish,
from the silky softness
of their songs,
from their eyes adorned
with vitreous sands,
the stillness of the temples and the gardens

(in their acanthus shadows, in the rocks
they touch and soften)

> they have opened their chambers
> they have laid their river-beds
> beneath the tepid leaves of the almond trees.

They speak about the texture
of their shining scales
about the tranquil games that slide toward the edge
of the slow shore of their sunsets.
About their icy lips.

Eyes of fine-grained stones.

About the foam that they hurl, and the aroma they pour

(In the atriums: the sails, the amaranths.)

Over the very light altar of their harvests.

Sediment of Lukewarm and Radiant Rain

"I sat down to remember
toward the end of the park
and the memory came to me
like a hunger fever,
but it was one of those memories that are peaceful
without people;
one of those memories that are not measured,
that are not told
and that do not know
about those that are obscured by so much light, and
empty from their greatness."
In the flame of time your voice is a burning field.
The days have passed like fish climbing upstream at night,
and ending up dead in the morning in the light of the valleys;
they have woven their nets
like lengthy vines,
like deep and contractible distances in the water.

And your voice, and your eyes
suddenly kindle
as if the wall, the surging tide, were none other
than that leaving behind of
the most definite immensity
in the habitual manner of half-closing eyes
or in any other tidal flow of tenderness;

Because your flame is ocean earth,
and in your night crowd together
– like the ebb and flow of the tides –
all the densities suspended
between a thread of death
and this pen that tapers itself to your silence;
silence of narrow eternity, of unarmed expansion.

Because watching you die is something my eyes cannot grasp
and freeing your arms from death
is like ripping apart a lake in two shores:
two magnets that pull at each other to break you.

I want to depart from you
as if swimming to the depths of your eyes and running
        into the shade
with your slow abyss of burning grass,
with your calm of extinquishable bird,
weak like the flesh.

Because I don't know what to do with so many of your gestures,
so much of your vision in my words,
I write so that they will burn
so that they will eradicate,
and uproot
this deer-like anxiety in your eyes,
that marine death rattle between your lips,
and so that they will return you to the circle of silence
of this deserted afternoon.

    "Beautiful park, beautiful children,
beautiful afternoon, but on the bench
there is an empty space."

Then it was easy to remember you; your words arose from a
reencounter barely suspended in an echo of willow trees.

    "It is as if in the parks the time that grieved you so, did
not flow, as if both, new thoughts and old memories, were
equally fresh and clear, serene and hopeful."

You voice was a road of overflowing ivy, and time, a slow
recount of future landscapes, of solitary illuminated waters.

    "There is also a river, narrow, in the depths,
but there are no willows along its shore;
or rocks to cross it,
or rocks to throw into it."

And I invented your eyes and half-opened your gaze like a children's
song that dissembowls the silence; because there already was silence
in that opening of the doors, in that scrutinizing of language that the
parks distend; a sound distinct from silence.

(Later, I became this surf, this abrupt and prolonged evidence, this living the sea in delicate, interrupted sips, that foamy sand of the barely touched, of the barely dissolved). And it was like the two of us having a piece of that same silence, that small gesture of the night that is like a mirror on the backs of the doors, like a premature fall in the abysmal uprising of the chords.

Your death surprises me in the sea with the closed eyes. It was like opening a murmur in that nude shadow of the willow trees, that awakens in its voice, like dawn does to the night, the language of salt that the surfs hurl into the daybreak. It was like the two of us waiting in a small room where the doors are time and mirrors; you talk about some dream where the waters overflow, drag the tides from the shore, and carry you away, like a final attempt to try to swim, to look for a way to wrench from the sea, from the silence, the distended ditch that receives your body. You talk about hallways, about attempting a return, and you don't find the room number. I vaguely see your voice multiplied by the echo of the mirrors. "Only numbers in close proximity." Your hands are the flames of a forest that extinguishes itself, like a murmur that sustains the heat of the night. Night is a reflection; your image is like an eternal saying yes, come, let me accompany you outside. There is a noise of lights gathering together.

"Only numbers in close proximity." Because the echo is the light of distance, and the room is a splendor of dampened earth, of salt element, of light and radiant sediment, like opening the faucet and putting the head under and suddenly, the sea is already a dark and passionate imminence, a deep murmur of lava that bursts from afar, from the depths, like a conflagration that grows from the waters.

Rain is a continuous time patrol;
Your voice, a soft and blind journey, a turning on the light,
a sudden raising of the floodgates of fire.

"Why then, the roots?"

A furtive grimace in the mirrors.
The room is a refuge of slow rain, of
ample and tenuous spaces,
of light riverbeds of reverberating voice.

A mirror of salt where the waters have dug an ebb tide of
agitated impulses; where night has dripped its estuary, slowly,

like an habitual omen.

In your lips;
    "In your eyes only sand,
soft sand."

So that they will eradicate, and uproot this deer-like anxiety.

    "Of those children I do not see," "how can the eyes of those
children I do not see be?"

Outside, the rain increases.

The walls have that virtual edge that distances them or shows
them with a fleeting outline of uncertain grass, with a sea-like
reflection.

                    Your space, warm and untouched.
Sometimes, fire arises from some slow and defeaned word;
then, I shut my eyes to the memory.

                    Translated by Celeste Kostopulos-Cooperman.

Elsa Cross

Elsa Cross was born in Mexico City in 1946. Her first eight books of poetry were collected in *Espejo al sol: Poemas, 1964-1981.* Cross' books *Baniano* (1986) and *Canto Malabar* (1987) were written in India. For her collection *El diván de Antar* (1990), she won the Aguascalientes National Prize for Poetry. Her most recent book of poems, *Casuarinas,* was published in 1992.

. . . .

Sri Nityananda Mandir
(The Temple of Nityananda)

He smiles from his statue.
Flames of the lamps
reflect on his breast
                            waving in circles.
Incense,
              camphor.
And the rain brings a scent of jasmine
to the window
          guarded by a cobra of clay.

(More fragrance in his hands.)

The chants begin.
Sparrows within the temple,
salamanders that glide over the wall —
and the sparrows quiet
                      as if listening

Vande jagat karanam

Cause of the world
Owner of the world
Form of the world
                    Destroyer—

He smiles from his statue
and in the nocturnal ablution
his head receives

---

rose water,
perfumes,
          rivers of milk and honey.

The curve of his shoulders trembles,
his eyes see
and his dark skin is warm.
His nearness,
          rapture.

Banyan

Aerial,
born in the heights,
the roots descend
          until they reach the earth.
They meet the font of their lineage,
the root of themselves.
They become foundation
          – column and arch –
lay out their labyrinths,
close grottos,
thicken under odors of pepper
brought by the same air
          that loosens the leaves,
live and smooth
as the plants of your feet.

Steps that glide without grazing the ground.

Kali

Her body is dark as Death;
eternity shines in her face.
— Ramprasad

Your fury explodes,
oh Mother.
A green radiance illuminates me.
You pulverize the fields, the flocks,
the white fences.
Everything spins.
Your ax pierces me.
My blood spurts
and on falling forms
worlds with their own direction.
My bones slit other strata.
My skull adorns your garland.
Oh Mother,
you are that which destroys
and that which is destroyed:
you are a bridge suspended between two ages.

Visions

1.

Sea of living silver
city of gold
amidst the leaves the stone face
is enthroned

footprints in the air
transparent feet

release from dark cocoons
their flight from silk
veils escaping

Uma Worshiping Shiva
(On a Kangra miniature)

— for Maria Jose and Octavio Paz

Within herself
she hears the voice resounding
in the narrow range
running from the crux of her hearing
to her dazzled brow.

The voice travels only a few notes,
loses modulation.
It strips the sound of cadence,
of rhythm,
strips each syllable of letters.

It is pure vibration,
arrow that climbs
— leap of monkey between branches —

and remains
in the infinite division of spaces
covering each ant's footprint,
each grain of sand on the shore.

Vibration
surging from itself
                sole current
without scale or quaver
without pause
                without echo
continual
          even now identical to silence
fixed flow —

       river of silver
on whose bank Uma sits.
The floor of her bamboo house
is covered with fresh leaves.
Uma writes.
The river unfolds like a canvas.
Uma smiles.
Her hair looks like a dark fish.
She has sprinkled flowers on the white stone
vertical to the white oval crosswise beneath.
To one side, parallel,
she has placed the written leaves.
She has another in her hand.
Uma writes with red ink
on mango leaves.
There is neither east nor west.
There is light without shadow while Uma writes.
Her skirt is of leaves.
                — absorbed
an instant
an eye she looks at with her eyes closed
that eye looks at her
that eye is that which looks
and is also the looked upon
                  the look
brilliant gem
          a thousand eyes cover her,

atom of light rotating on itself.

Outside
        the sun passes between the trees.
The river plays in its banks.
A scent of jasmine
        lingers on Uma's forehead.
A drop of honey descends to her throat.

Uma dressed in leaves,
seated before the white stone.

Translated by Patricia Dubrava.

Rosita Kalina

Rosita Kalina, born in 1932 in Costa Rica, is the author of *Cruce de niebla* (1977) and *Detrása de las palabras* (1983). She is a professor of English literature at the University of San Andres in Costa Rica

. . . .

Dayeinu — they said
after wetting their little finger
ten times with wine
and leaving stains
— red drops —
on the white Easter tablecloth.

Happy, I repeated — *Dayeinu.*
I counted to ten
with my little finger
spattering the immaculate
tablecloth with red.

Childhood of lascerated grins
the lugubrious laments of Easter
resound like flagellums of war!

Never! Never will I return to childhood
to the vile age of innocence!

> *Dayeinu, dayeinu*
> Since I was a young girl I listened
> to this ancient word:
> Enough already!

Dayeinu: Enough already.

Testimonies

"And he said to me: Son of man,
can these bones live? And I anwered,
"O Lord God, thou knowest."
— Ezekiel 37-3

I

To the Prophet, Ezekiel

What ash rises high
in the valley of the Transfiguration?
What bones, what softness
buried yesterday
shapes live and
yerning skeletons?

It rises in flight
with a wheel of a thousand eyes
without knowing if in the beyond
there is only solitude or fright.

The captives no longer cry.
In the wings: a thousand eyes
nurish their tears.

And they rise up from the grave.

To Ezekiel, the Avenger

Why do you punich
and then comfort us?
It would be better for you to keep silent.
If we are to blind
to see your Temple,
leave us with our bindness
and continue with your vengeance.

We never were killers

and it's better that the smoke of the altar
be white.
You never told us that one day
there would be chimneys of black smoke
or altars to incinerate us.

What do you know, poet
of the clean hands?
If yesterday your children drank mud
from the sewers, while you
washed your vestments in the Quebar

I don't want your fragile anathema
Don't scream "Sablanut" at me.
My ears are deaf
from the noise of the pipes.
My eyes cry
in the fire of the ovens.

To Ezekiel, the Visionary

Your words return to you.
Broken hands will recover
their dignity
in the Age of Man.
Inscrutable judgments
save God.
Grief conquers grief
so that we can find
each other
in the valley of justice.

Why cry?

Translated by Celeste Kostopulos-Cooperman

Sablanut: Patience

Cecilia Vicuña

Cecilia Vicuña (Chile, 1948) is a poet, filmmaker, and painter. One of the most interesting figures in Latin American art and poetry, she has lived in New York City for the past twenty years. Her works include *Precareo* (1988), *Palabramar* (1970) and *Unravelling Words and the Weaving of Water*.

. . . .

from *Palabrarmás*

I saw a word in the air
solid and suspended
showing me
her seed body

She opened up and fell apart
and from her parts sprouted
sleeping thoughts
                    of love, livid
                                    in love, living
                                    out of love
came madder violet

Enchanting me
nipples and cupolas
chanting in me

She ascends in a spiral
as I fall in the break
between chant and cupola

In and out
of deserted palaces I wander
seeing the image of chanting
and entering
the beginning
                    the end
                            the word

The fractal image has thighs,
hips and wounds

to enter

She is mother and wind
her lean body
stalks and waits

She seeks
the door
whistling in love
pushing it
with a terse blow as
the door rolls
    in place

No one will see the same palace
once the threshold has been crossed
no one will see the same flowers
except through the gift
of ubiquity

Coincidence is a miracle
of chance, the crossing
of two vectors,
carelessly placed perhaps

Each word
awaits the traveler
hoping to find
in her
trails and suns
of thought

They wait
singing in silence
one hundred times touched
and changed
exhausted for a moment
and then revived

Lost or abandoned
they shine again

Celestial bodies
each
in its orbit

Quartz structure
sensed by touch
and the inner ear

body music
forms transform
born to die
enjoying
their conjugation

Space
that we penetrate

Lords of pen
in trance

Lords of words
or do they
love our works?

Do they
desire us as we
desire them?

Translated by Suzanne Jill Levine.

Alejandra Piznarnick

Alejandra Pizarnick (1936-1972) was without a doubt one of the most innovative voices of contemporary Latin American lyric. Her works merge dreams and vigil, exhibiting a profound concern for language at its purest simplicity. Among her most outstanding works are *Tierra Más Ajena* (1955), *La Ultima Inocencia* (1956), *Arbol de Diana* (1962), *Los Trabajos y Las Noches* (1965), *Extracción de la Piedra de la Locura* (1968) and her last book *El Infierno Musical*. To date, only one critical text in English has been published about Pizarnick's work, *Alejandra Pizarnick: A Portrait* by Frank Graziano.

. . . .

from *Tree Of Diana*

I.

I gave the surge of myself to the dawn.
I left my body joined with the light
while I sang out the sadness of being born.

II.

These are the versions offered to us:
a hole, a trembling wall . . .

III.

just thirst
silence
no meeting

care for me my love
care for the silent woman in the desert
the travelling woman with the empty cup
and the shadow of her shadow

VI.

she takes off her clothes in the paradise
of her memory

she is unaware of the harsh fate
of her visions
she is afraid of not being able to name
the non-existent

VII.

Leaping with her shirt in flames
from star to star,
from shadow to shadow.
Dying a distant death
the woman in love with the wind.

IX.

These bones gleaming in the night,
these words like precious stones
in the live throat of a petrified bird,
this much loved green-ness,
this warm lilac,
this lonely mysterious heart.

XIV

The poem I do not write,
the one I do not deserve.
Fear of being two
pathways in a mirror:
someone sleeping within me
eats me and drinks me.

Recognition

You made the silence of lilacs swaying
in the tragic breezes of my heart.
You made my life a tale for children
where deaths and shipwrecks
are pretexts for splendid parties.

Shadow of Days to Come

Tomorrow
they will clothe me in ashes at dawn
they will fill my mouth with flowers.
I will learn to sleep
with the memory of a wall
with the breathing
of an animal that dreams.

Foundation Stone

I cannot speak with my voice but with my voices.

His eyes were the entrance to the temple for me, wandering here loving and dying. And I would have sung until I became one with night, until I stood naked at the start of time.

I go through that song like a tunnel.

Disturbing presences,
gestures of shapes that seem to be alive through
the vital language that names them,
signs which strike uncalmable terror.

A tremble in the cement, a quiver in the foundations, drains, bores through, and I have come to know where she stays, that other being which is myself, waiting for me to become silent to take me over and drain me, bore through my cement, my foundations,

the one who is my opposite, plotting to occupy my waste land

no,
        I must do something
no,
        I must do nothing.

Something in me cannot give in to the ashes which rain down, which well up inside the woman who is me, with me being her and being myself, unspeakably separate from her. In the sameness of silence (not in the same silence) swallowing night, a vast night steeped in the secrecy of lost footsteps.

I cannot speak to say nothing. We lose ourselves that way, the poem and I, in a useless attempt to write out burning feelings.

Where will this writing lead? To darkness, to sterility, to fragmentation.

Dolls, torn to pieces by my ancient doll-like hands, the disappointment of feeling raw stuffing inside (raw steppes, your memory); a father, who wanted to be Tiresias, floating in the river. But you, why did you let them kill you as you listened to stories of snow white poplar trees?

With those doll-like fingers of mine, I wanted to really feel the keys. I did not want to skim along the keyboard like a spider. I wanted to sink in, dive deeply, fix myself, solidify. I wanted to become part of the keyboard, so as to enter into music and get myself a homeland. But music moves, it hurries along. Only when a refrain repeated itself, did I feel inside myself the slight hope of being able to establish something like a train station. I mean, a firm, sure point of departure, a place from which to leave, from the place, to the place, at one and together with the place. But the refrain was so short that I could not set up a station, I could only count on one, somewhat derailed train, that coiled and uncoiled. Then I gave up music and its betrayals, because music was more above or more below, but not in the center, in the place of blending and meeting. (You who were my only homeland, where could I look for you? Perhaps inside the poem I write.)

One night in the circus I recovered a lost language in the instant when riders with torches in their hands galloped round fiercely, mounted on black steeds. In my dreams of happiness could there exist a choir of angels that could offer my heart anything comparable to the burning sounds of hoofbeats against the sand.

(And I say to myself: Write: because these words are honest and true.)

(Poetry begins with a man or a stone or a tree . . .)

And there was a softly quivering tremor (I say this to instruct her, the one who lost her musicality in me and trembled with more disonnance than a horse driven wild by a torch on the sands of a foreign land).

I was embracing the ground, speaking a name. I believed I had died and that death was saying a name without end.

Perhaps this is not what I want to say. This saying and being named is not welcome. I cannot speak with my voice but with my voices. Sometimes a poem may be a trap door, one more scenario.

When the ship shifted its rhythm and vacillated on rough waters, I stood there like an Amazon, who can tame a rearing horse just with her blue eyes (or was it just with her blue eyes?). The green water in my face, I need to drink of you until night opens. Nobody can save me because I am invisible even to the me who calls with your voice. Where am I? I am in a garden.

There is a garden.

Fragments to Overcome Silence

The strongest parts of language are lonely, desolate women, singing out through my voice which I hear in the distance. And far away, lying on black sand, is a girl filled with ancestral music. Where is real death? I wanted to illuminate myself in the light of my lack of light. Branches die in my memory. The girl nestles down in me with her she-wolf's mask. She who could go on no longer and pleaded for flames and we burned together.

2

When the roof is blown off the house of language and words cannot heal, I speak. The women in red are lost behind their masks though they still go back to sob among the flowers. Death is not voiceless. I hear the mourners chanting as they seal the cracks in silence. I hear your gentle weeping blossom in my grey silence.

3

Death has restored to silence the status of enchantment. And I will not recite my poem, and I must recite it. Even though (here, now) the poem has no meaning, has no destiny.

Suspicion

Mother used to tell us about a white forest in Russia . . . "and we'd make little snowmen and put hats on them that we took from great-grandfather . . ."

I would look at her with suspicion. Whatever was snow? Why make men out of it? And above all, what was a great-grandfather?

Poem For My Father

And then it was
that with his cold, dead tongue in his mouth
he sang the song they never let him sing
in this world of obscene gardens, of shadows
      that came abruptly to remind him
      songs from his time of boyhood
he, who never could sing the song he aspired to sing
the song they never let him sing
except through his absent blue eyes
his absent mouth
his absent voice.
Then, from the highest tower of absence
his song rang out through the gloom of concealment
through the silent spaces
filled with uneasy hollows like these words I write.

Speaking Your Name

Not a poem on your absence
just a sketch, a crack in a wall,
something in the wind,
a taste of bitterness.

Translated by Susan Bassnett.

Mercedes Roffé

Mercedes Roffé was born in Buenos Aires in 1954. She holds a degree in Modern Literatures from the University of Buenos Aires and a Ph.D. in Spanish from New York University. She has published three books of poetry: *Poemas 1973-1975, El Tapiz de Ferdinand Oziel,* and *Cámera baja palabras.* Her work has appeared in literary journals in Argentina, Spain, and in translation in the U.S. and Canada. She has lived in the U.S. since 1985 and currently teaches at Vassar College in Poughkeepsie, New York.

.. . .

A landscape of return is drawn
Voices
National language   the music
of the spheres
Perhaps because of being in the air
Because of being
            in flight
Because of being
            in return transit
Transit
            Synagogue of the
Tiny catalogue of the tribe
            Ceuta
            Tangers
            Oran
The narrow prison
the bracelets
the myth of the Moors and the songs
The intersection: seven languages
Casablanca:
            the end of a story I don't know
            how to tell or stop telling
Oran:
            the name that circumcises that which is
            uncircumcisable
Without the A there won't be concerts
            but Solos
Transit
Landscape of return

The angel comes to transfix a lung addicted
        to the literary tradition
                not only
The plastered tradition of a convent
You confuse a room with a convent
        the same
as your
        daughter's
        mother's
        grandmother's house
Orthopedia

Wanted

The mirror
Your fate on paper
A convent, she wants
A white enclosure in which
to be
        crossed
        transfixed
        married to
Father and master
Lyrist
        sing to me
        tell me
                make me
        endow me
        cover me
He who fears the lyre
        the music of the spheres
Won't not arrive
Oblique panorama
Father
        Mother

Uncle
        Aunt
                Aunt
What do I do here?
Run away to a party
Party
        fast!
                Party
Remember me
  It's me
        I'm here
Without gods there is no feast
Such a . . .
        Such a . . .
Mesié Fifí!
        Mesié Fifí!
Oh flame of love
The king dies
The king has died
Long live the king

It's not about being
It's not about being like you are
It's about
        photographing well
It doesn't make a difference to have waxed
It doesn't make a difference to have
        your cavities filled
It doesn't make a difference to weigh
        measure
        be
        more than
        less than
A play of light
The shadows
good paper
It doesn't pay to have the eyes of the sirens
It doesn't pay
        to speak
        until the sailors are driven crazy

It doesn't pay
to have thrown yourself out the window last night
        where there is no glass: interrupted
        faintings
It's about coming out well
like in a shipwreck

Thou shalt not worship false idols
Thou shalt not utter my name in vain
Thou shall adore false idols without uttering
        their name
until your house becomes a labyrinth
In the blessing of Abraham
        your name was written
A dandy
        a young man
        a Jewish girl
        a dancer from Argel
                Arnaut Daniel
        Johnny
        Brunilda
        Isabel Freyre

The Lighthouse of Alexandria

Yes, the time
yes
Two years
There couldn't be rites without time
Time to laugh and time to cry
Time to blaspheme and time
        to read the prophets

There wouldn't be rites if not
like today
Today makes
Today would make
They say
      the mothers
      the girlfriends of the dead
Then
 Now
What has become of you
      my creeper
To whom are you said to be

Time to discover each other and time to lose each other
Time of birds and time
      of crossroads
There won't be rites if
A season does not come and go
      my candid sun on a cold day
face of sun
      face of country and milk
      kale hemera for your eyes
      kale hemera
            for the sigh of the river
Who will cultivate those corals
Who will collect those corals
      from the water beds.
The tablets, do you remember?
"There was another first day"
There was
      the blood of another woman
      then mine
Who will collect them
Who will remember them
Who
      will orchestrate the Allelujah

Translated by Kathryn Kopple.

Gestures From My Window

Blanca Wiethüchter

Blanca Wiethüchter (1942) is one of the young and innovative poets of Bolivian lyric. She is also a literary critic and professor at the University of La Paz. Her books include *Madera Viva* (1982) and *Arbol Di Junio* (1989).

. . . .

Without Histories

1.

We who are responsible for living
and have been born in the third world.

We who ask for justice
and live in South America.

We who die in Bolivia
disconsolate and alone

we are the history that cannot be written
and journey with the head cut off.

2.

A student is killed by a shot in the back.

The spilled blood
spreads over the street
like a cry.

Who could write about innocence?

Song

Among the clamor the single shout
the transparency
receives the only cipher:
the reason for the real movement
           one plus one
           is four
           not three.

At This Juncture

When the night has already turned
to the core of voices
and the distant barking to accomplices
of the circular moon and the open eye.

When stripped
of many decisions
I find myself always
with the same desires
with the same profound currents,
the body impregnated with the splendor
of every beat.

In full invention of myself
I feel strong
immensely uncertain
having chosen already
forgiveness
to walk and drink life in.

When the living has spilled
into an invisible grimace
with the vision of the first deaths,
I have only learned
this devotion
matured in smallness
that ties me infallibly
to everything alive.

Movement

1.

Multiples in the looks of fright
clouded in the privilege of solitude
we lose the voice's certainty
abandon the act in suspicion.

We are not empty spectators in life
but tremulous actors and for only one time:
to return to the precise question
to the ignorant innocence
to the lucidity that discovers the aggressors
at the foot of the others.

The day will come
for the anguished that endure the wound.
The day will come
for the joyful to break the habit.
The day will come
for those isolated from man.

2.

Time passes
swiftly
we have lost so much life
already.

Man is the blade and the knife
man is the dark key
of the first and last radiance.

Tear off the mask
look at the sun among the blood
the air among the asphyxia
look at the water among the rain.
Invent ourselves equal and new
in this our only hour.

3.

Memory of love
opens our embrace.
Desire for stillness
that permits our raving
invents our light.

Beneath the light of the only adventure
the splendor is conceived:
an open world
shares its fruits equally.

Translated by Shaun T. Griffin and Emma Sepúlveda-Pulvirenti.

Romelia Alarcoñ de Folgar

Romelia Alarcoñ de Folgar (1920-1970) was born in Guatemala City in the 1920s. She was both a poet and journalist. Among her works are *Claridad* (1960), and *Tiempo Inmovil* (1965).

. . . .

Irreverent Epistle to Jesus Christ

Christ,
come down from your cross and wash your hands.
wash your knees and your side,
comb your hair,
put on your sandals
and blend your footsteps
with all the footsteps that are searching for you
on the mountain ranges and the sea,
over the land;
through the air,
along the wire fences of the roads.

You can solve anything,
everything's easy for you
and so . . .
what are you waiting for?
Why don't you come down from your cross right now?
Without parables, with bullets
and loose reefs sharp with vengeance
in your hands . . .

And let the towns be filled with freed men
and midday sun,
orchards, doves and roses
their petals still full bloom
and bugles that announce
peaceful mornings.

Christ,
come down from your cross
where thousands of men
hang crucified beside you:

wash your hands and their hands,
your knees and their knees,
your side and their sides;
wash your forehead and their foreheads
crowned with thorns.

Don't let your impassive martyrdom continue:
show your wrath,
come down from your cross,
mingle with the men who love you.

Monday

Monday has the long face
of the sweat
and the smell of closed factories

Nevertheless;
Monday streets bathed in joyful light
resound in happy tunes
with throngs of workers and saws,
nails and wood.
Architects and bricklayers
all working together as equals
go from one level to the next
with long crystal balconies
and young doors made of fragrant wood
thinking about the sprouts in the jungle.

The ilex and the oak become chests
and carved panels.
Man smiles on Monday
and smooths out flowers of cement.
The hours of Monday

accumulate like coins
in pockets
and then bouquets of personal dreams
blossom.

The day slowly undresses,
hour by hour,
and is left naked at twelve o'clock
until the sound of whistles
shatters the wind.
Clusters of rough hands
and bunches of vigilant eyes
making their living
with accustomed skill
hold down their jobs
with fixed roots.

Suddenly,
a flurry of footsteps
on the sleepers laid that afternoon
and Monday
puts on the white face of the stars.

Panorama

I

It's useless
it's no longer possible to ask
in simple words, how are you friend?
and to speak in the manner of a poet.

Then clots of blood
mix together
larvae begin to stir
the skin-deep gash
the howl drags through the wind
chapters of moist eyelides
and frightful moans.

One can no longer talk in an ordinary voice
about anything that is beautiful
take for instance the rain in July
with its shining foliage and fragrant purpose
and hundreds of birds
and genders of violets.
Then corpses jump out
and heads with no torsos.

The voice is an enraged call
wavering in the fog.
There are demons bellowing on Sundays,
and spectres drinking the light
it is no longer possible to speak as before
in the manner of a poet
this is now the "city of tears."

But perhaps some day
the good gods of the past
will come with renewed men
and gentle rivers
along the roads of the homeland
bleached by the sun.

Panorama II

Today I woke up again
in my same old way of living
and going out onto the street
with my briefcase full of papers.

As always with glasses
to observe more sweetly
anything around me
including
the wind pushing hours
in its dazzling wheelbarrow.

I like to live
up to my eyes
in the bustle of the day.
To touch its infinite belly
— population of glowworms —
its thigh made of trees
its feet of fine moss
its face of transparent leaves
and to walk poised
on fragrances.

From time to time
a trill resounds.
From time to time a lost light
falls on my hands
covering them like gloves.

And the changing architecture of a cloud marches by
like a pattern of doves,
and birds stack up
and gateways to space,
while I walk
and turn to some new song
in my same old way of living.

Protest

Why remember that I am a poet
and that wild flowers
grow daily on my chest.

In the enclosed circle of the day
any sound touches my heart
and even the asphalt on the streets frightens me.

A few weeks ago I wrote a poem
a son of mine made of the earth and the sky
I sent him to the newspaper,
I have heard no more of him
he is out of focus.

Maybe he is lost
amongst a bundle of papers
that talk about murders,
the raped girl,
politics, expensive lives
and many other things where there is no room
for either a rose or love.

He, that son of mine, was only carrying
by way of provisions a handful of grass
and a few odd stars
in his pockets.

Because
it was
poor equipment
he would feel defenseless and alone
he was lacking a dagger and a machine gun.

Poetry is in exile
nobody wants anything to do with her.
Her plumed robes
are useless
if there are unburied men
abandoned on the streets.

Nocturnal

Every night death counts on her fingers
while she consumes cigarettes:
Every night she visits bedrooms and smiles.

Something withers every night
within the body;
something is taken away from the heart and falls
with scarcely a sound.

And waters cut by scales
create changing mirrors
that reflect dead faces.

Every night death goes about her work freely
and time becomes slim:
glass belts break
and lights go out.

Let's talk about today
with the certainty of the light tomorrow
with the certainty of the encounter.

And on each corner an angel
with a box of matches
to light up the dawn.

All of the wind rests on altars
that sustain its image
all of the wind . . .

Every night we cover the same distances
— the dream is an island —.
Every night a fistful of laughter is lost.

Every night
death counts on her fingers
and extinguishes roses.

Translated by Alison Ridley.

Yolanda Bedregal

Yolanda Bedregal was born in La Paz, Bolivia, in 1916, and studied art and art history at its Academía de Bellas Artes. She later continued her studies at Barnard College in New York City and returned to Bolivia to teach aesthetics and art history at the University of Saint Andrew, the Conservatory of Music, and the Academía de Bellas Artes. As the author of many volumes of poetry, short stories, novels and travel writing, she has won many of her nation's most important literary prizes and has exhibited her own sculptures as well. She is the widow of poet Gert Conitzer and still lives in La Paz with her two children.

. . . .

Martyrdom

The retina fills with skies and expanses of grass,
neglected seas slip through the eyes,
and one drowns in the vast solitude of oneself,
> bound to the hours
> and nailed to the earth.

Gestures From My Window

The black night spies upon my window
like the eye lying in wait for darkness.

It's as if thick night were being gnawed
by a tooth that concealed its howl of laughter.
Perhaps my window is a golden tear
that will moisten the night from within my room.

Is it not a knife-thrust from the silences
which leaves a fresh wound upon the shadow
and makes the lights in my window bleed?

Intact Pitcher

for Humberto Viscarra Monje

Today I have drunk the sun through every pore,
but its joy didn't reach me.

This sun of the high plateau in winter
in a wide blue cup of grassy satin
filtered its poison drop by drop
like a slow reproach.

It's just that I have so much night in my soul
that the day resents me.

Who could be an empty pitcher,
virgin clay,
to be filled with grains of gold!

Who could be broken,
spilled into shadows,
and re-reformed as amphora,
round, smooth, intact!

May the sun pour into her,
and may her musical key adorn
blond assurance in the hollow of the soul!

Pointless Journey

Why the sea?
　　　Why the sun!
　　　　　Why the sky?
I'm on a journey today,
on a journey of return

toward that word without a shore
which is the sea of myself
and of forgetting you.

After I had given you sea and sky,
I remain with the earth of my life
which is sweet as clay
drenched in blood and milk.

Now all that I had is excess
because I am like an aquarium and like a rock.
Agile fish sail through my blood,
and in my body the roots of violet
and yellow plants are entangled.

I have on my wounded shoulder
scars of useless wings,
and in my eyes still there is
a little pointless moisture of recollections.

But what does all this matter now?
When I stretch out my arms there is nothing
that is not myself repeated.
Am I not perchance the sea, am I not rock?

Mysteries of colors in my life
rise and fall in high tidal surges,
and strange animals and demons
pretend to be angels and ferns in my caverns.

They're all too much, the sea, the sun, the earth.

Now that I have returned from an unbounded love,
I have already in the word without a shore
what once could fit within his hands.

Nocturne of Hope

Night is a ship of mother-of-pearl and gold
that furrows sleep's ocean with the clean
and purified breeze of fear.

Night is the refuge, a return
to the dark breast where life remains
a kernel of unnameable hope.

I love the night in which I wheel, minimal
as a tiny skein of blood becalmed.

I love the night in which I die a little
and am greatly born in the unsheared fleece of shadows.

I love this sinking into everything,
                        nothing to nothing,
this magnificent fall into the ocean
of crystalline shadows gathered
in a hollow so much my own and so other.

I love the night, larva of mystery,
elliptic quietude, unnumbered seed.
I am very small to be awake.
I want to return to the egg of night!

Night, I Know All About You

Skin of the night bristling with stars,
what tormented rivers of light
will make of your darkness their refuge?
You are an enormous woman with closed eyes,
and your skin shudders with morning stars
dreaming of the day

that exists beneath your shadow-dimmed flesh.

I know, night, all about you because my skin
which has sensed you for a long time in its sleeplessness,
is made, like you, of shadow, and illumined
by the warm rivers of your arms.

I know, night, about you who are of ash,
because I am ash illuminated.
If the day touches you, you are consumed;
if its soul touches me, I revive.

You, half of yourself; I, half of myself.
You of shadow, I of ash
we are constellated of tears and kisses
with the round embrace of sleep that completes us.

Night, your skin of light bristles;
my skin of spirit iridesces
drinking from your flesh the milk of stars.

My soul drinks from the body its joy,
and you drink light from the darkness.

Poppies

Purple sleep of the golden wheatfield,
silk crushed under the light footstep
of sleepless angels,
what sensual nostalgias pierced you
with blood almost black in a green mouth?

The color in you rehearses its arpeggios
when you dress yourself from deep scarlet to white:

bride's veil in frothy folds;
petticoat inflamed with ruffled selvages;
puffed, rounded velvet
of funerary mantle
or Lenten pall.

Poppy

Flags aloft in the wind
when the hooves of light
trot through mid-day's epic pastures;
lamps of pallid dawn
when the earth gives birth
and the mothers groan in their pain;
poppy blossomed in the sheets
of the wedding night;
poppy bending over the wheat spear's cradle
like a canopy that distills millenary stories
over the uncertain germs;
poppy rotting over the corpses
cut down by war.

Today
in the glass on my table,
startled from transported sleep.

Tomorrow
little green skulls crowned
in a sea of fallen petals . . .

Oh poppies!

Blood of vegetal sleep,
sleep of vegetal blood,
like life: Blood and sleep.

Poppies, oh poppies!

Translated by Carolyne Wright.

Laura Riesco

Laura Riesco (Lima, Perú, 1939) is an outstanding Peruvian author. Her acclaimed novel, *El Truco de los Ojos*, is considered to be one of the most innovative narratives by a Peruvian writer. She is presently a professor at the University of Orono in Maine.

. . . .

So You Would Listen to Me

So you would listen to me
I tangled your silence

My words became
shrill with the wind

The starry shadows
of all my poems
plunged in your eyes

So you would listen to me
God put you in the night

The whole world put
solitude in our steps

So you would listen to me
I diverted your path

How many nights spent
I gave you in a minute

You were to blame
for the tremor of my hands

You were to blame
and now you listened to me

Illuminated knives
crossed my breasts

I dug from the cavity
the reason of my dreams

So you would listen to me
I tangled your silence

I was falling in parts
and in parts in silence
I was leaving the soul to you.

Burdens

They enter without calling by the false door.
Barefoot, noiseless, they come close
and they break
the tranquil order of our place.

They parody the laughter and roll it over
in terrible wry faces
through a friendly floor that does not know us.
They squeeze, voracious, blood out of the furniture.
They change into an image of sorrowful monsters
the face learned from childhood
in our mirrors.
They take the bad thoughts to the air
secretly sweeping them beneath the rugs.
They twist the skins of the sweet children
and they go about turning them to sad elders.

They enter and they remain.
They prohibit the sun, draw the curtains.
They forbid all of our doors with a bolt
in order to start the nightmare
a dance of shadows.
(Drop by drop they add thick, black coffee
to our sleeplessness.)

We begin succumbing to their dictates.
Their spiritless hands, now eyes without sight
we corner ourselves in the small hands
of a clock without motion.

When I Passed in the Afternoon

I saw him.
When I passed in the afternoon
with my basket of thoughts
When my hair still had
the odor of his hands
and my body vibrated
with reddened caresses

When the world smiled
When the grass shone
When my sorrows left
astonished
and a song of praise
broke in my veins

When the hour of being
seemed more beautiful to me
When I had lowered the head
as a sign of eternal surrender
When there was no fear
in the memory

I saw him.
      He smiled and it was not mine
      his smile.
Alas! When I passed in the afternoon.

Translated by Shaun T. Griffin and Emma Sepúlveda-Pulvirenti.

Eunice Odio

Eunice Odio (1947) is a Costa Rican poet who lived throughout the countries of Central America, most particularly Guatemala where she spent many years. She was living in Mexico at the time of her death in 1974. Her principal works include *Los elementos terrestres* (1948) and *Territorio del alba* (1946-1954).

. . . .

from *In the Life and Death of Rosamel Del Valle*

> To Teresa Dulac, the Hardworking Angel,
> the angelic wife of Rosamel

I.

It is not true that you are far from "the light that can find you.."
That would make us outlaws;

that would be

taking us away from what calls us in torrents
and walks abundantly
and hurls itself skyward toward the threshold of the gods.

It is not true that you are far from where it can find us
a voice that chooses us from among all the animals in the world and says:

Here, you, those who are similar to the grass!
It is not true that you are far
from this crystal that submerges my hands among its waves,
that takes them away in the vision of the water,
while I drink with glittering sips.

It is not true . . . Because today Teresa, and you and I
were listening to the sound of the butterfly awakening and we said:
here is the nakedness of she who has dreamed . . .
Of all those who are awake, inside the wings
And the Someone came to us with a crystalline face
and dizzy wings.

saying words like endless fields.

And we were afraid . . . With his hand on his heart
looking at us without any eyes, attentively and tumultuously,
until the last glass of blood;
and full of happiness, poured into the great river,
whose torrents gave and took away
animals and skies and fountains of water.

IV.

It is the dawn.
Teresa, Hardworking Angel, leave your watch at the river!
It is the dawn of a day with power over all the four cardinal points.
It is now time to leave.
Teresa, put on the dress which the fishermen prefer;

Put on your wings so that you may fly, Teresa;
in order to fly with the speed of a soul;

and before that, put on the cloak sent to you by the Spring.

Orpheus, tell the day to fly quickly

from *Creation*

II.

I'm at the point of hurting myself and listening to myself
Now I propose an equation to the dust
for the slitting away of my throat,

Now that I inaugurate my return
next to my illuminated smallness,

Now that I search for myself revealed
and broken down into other names,

When for my sake there descend and regroup
thick temperatures of the morning,

and the deer celebrate a great feast on the roads.

III.

My heart passes by
with its soft and painful identity.

I raise up high my transitive breath
and the child whose steps prolong me.

But my blood is already moving,
it reverberates,
toward a recondite and steady country,
between heavy irons that hear the name of a boy,
and extensive materials outside my own pulse.

My blood is already moving
toward a part of my being to which I will soon arrive,   ¡
and it knows the breast on which I stumble,
and the extensive, pallid, northern arteries of my heart.

My body is already filled with lily blossoms
as a season of the branch in its own efficacy;
a solitary palace on whose shore
the earth rises and flows in between flocks of animals
and in between secret and peaceful dreams.

IV.

My wandering breath can pass by,
my instantaneous hair
and my atrocious rapidity that doesn't catch up with me,
But my weight of the recovered inhabitant
has once again become inaugural

And winds of birth summon me,

Ah, happy group of bones in repose!

They flow in my being and congregate
soft and earthly elements
and the flesh now denied and running off.

The birds transport me
to higher states of sound,

And the earth to thrusts of flat prairie.

I am at the point of hurting myself and listening to myself
Now I fill myself with shoots of plants and tranquil eyelids,

When I am accustomed to being born
where temporal bones descend,

When I call to myself in a quiet voice,
and someone who is not me now remembers me,

Sobbing and bleeding half way,
above what has been detained
discovered
and recovered.

Translated by Arthur Natella.

Magda Portal

The work of the Peruvian Magda Portal (1903-1989), who was one of the most active participants in APRA, "Alianza Popular Revolucionaria Americana," is characterized by powerful political activism. The majority of her works are written in prose. Among her most outstanding collections are *Flora Tristrán Precursora* (Lima, 1945), *Hacia La Mujer Nueva* (Lima, 1933), and *Una Esperanza al Mar* (1927) Her work as a poet has only recently become known.

. . . .

Thirst for the Sea

Distant sea, memory
beach gilded with sun,
your sand knows my torment,
breeze of spring, love-breeze.

Wide road, the widest
for my longing to travel,
all the routes in your country,
open arms, wide sea.

In you the heart feels
free, serene and strong,
for you life loves life
and love also loves.

Take me, sea, take me far,
to a path without end,
lull me to sleep in your womb
with the last happy dream.

Attitude

I am quiet, like this, stubbornly quiet
face to the night, face to the dead moon and the stars,
and face to the sea, I am always quiet,
I have such fear of words!

They come headlong, like torrents they come
the blue words, the red, the violet,
and capsize their anguish and tarnish dawn,
and they open like wounds with no blood.

A secret fright disturbs me, but how would I
be able to tell someone of this coming death,
tell it, but run from it, road walked and unwalked,
question without answer, desolate look.

A round of light steps but sure steps,
where are your visible prints leading me?
if my hands do not ask nor my eyes worry
my overflowing anguish seizes still.

World round and alone, I would go around you,
I would go to the people for whose love I live still,
I would take their rhythm, their ingenuous innocence
and the smile would return to my face.

But each time I leave feeling more foreign,
more distant and absent and foreboding comes near
no more pain, no more love, no more anguish,
but no longer will I feel foreign.

Like a collision with oneself
the stripping of all that is unnecessary,
the useless vanity and desires, and the fear,
and the love, the pleasure, the ambition, the feeling.

And like this, cleansed of bonds, of ties, of ballast
freely ascend like in a dream without fantasy,
night of folding wings, the stars will illumine
my final hour of exile.

Watch of Time

Today is a day like any other,
by chance do they sell happiness at the fair?
The fireflies have disappeared
and in the sky dark seaweed floats.

And one time I had the simple light
of clear friendship and of the roses,
and the drowsy voices of the sea
in the harmonious distances.

I had! – like a tight bundle
they were the attributes of the first age
and smile of green emeralds
and the flush of spring.

Did I not drink the golden honey
and bitterness bit my young lip?
and the swords crossed me
in a rite without name.

Night tore dark branches
from my closed garden in mid-day,
carried away by the north wind
my voice cried without end, without moderation.

Death arrived with its heavy suit
of pale, silent stars
and dressed my elusive words
of roses white and roses red.

The time comes and goes so fast without calming
and catches me unchanged and tied down,
sleep falls in the tanned face
and in the eyes the look penetrates.

And over the wide world night falls,
and this space is filled with waves,
a boyish cry breaks the crystals
and rises slowly toward the light.

Translated by Shaun T. Griffin and Emma Sepúlveda-Pulvirenti.

Rosario Ferré

Rosario Ferré (1942) is one of the most innovative and important voices of Puerto Rican short story writing and poetry. Her principle works are *Papeles de Pandora* (1976) and *Fábulas de la garza desangrada* (1984). She presently lives in San Juan.

. . . .

Opprobium

My name is Antigone: I was buried alive
by those who owed obedience to the tyrant,
by those who, threatened with fear,
entrusted their heavy orchards, laden with golden fruit
to his care.With the moon of my menses
I wove the shroud in which I burn, unblemished
at the dregs of my death.
Centuries have gone by and my blood
still betrays me: it pours out of my wounds
each time a rebel dares to curse the satrap.

Message

To my mother,
and to my mother's monument,
to my aunts,
and to their well bred manners,
to Martha,
as well as to Mary,
because she dared choose the better part,
to Francesca, the immortal one,
because from deepest Hell
she insists on praising love's agony,

to Catherine, who unravels over water
the pristine obscenities of her ecstasy
as she strums upon the axe's whistle,
to Rosario, and to Rosario's shadow,
to the Erynnies and to the Furies
who, locked in amorous strife,
mourned and sang by her cradle,
to all those who agreed to condescend
I address the completion of these verses.
Because I sing,
because I sew and shine and ache and rearrange
the ever changing order of my bones
because I cry and trace
o'er my goblet's vanished breath
the humors of my human borne experience,
I name myself my own hand's irate foe
as I avenge destiny's misfortune.
Because I still live,
and am,
and hesitate to silence
my obstinately crimsoned lips,
because I still laugh
and keep my promises
and love
to iron
amongst all of us
the tiniest creases of my chaos
I ring out today in praise of joy and glory.

Translated by Rosario Ferré

You Have Lost, They Tell Me, Your Reason

you have lost, they tell me, your reason
hear me well

when you go down the street
everyone points a finger at your cocked head
as if they wanted to blow it off you
only pull the trigger and boom!
your forehead caves in on you like a beer can

don't say hello to anyone
don't comb your hair, don't shine your shoes
cross the street on your own arm
take your own hand, button your collar
stay alert

there goes the crazy man, they say

you go bobbing by your dusty head
like a wooden saint taken out for a parade
your feet nailed to the worm-eaten platform
looking in the distance
don't let your flesh ripen
let yourself be stoned

you have lost, it is evident, your reason
listen well

tie yourself tightly to the mast
bind yourself to the polar star
don't unhinge the ancient planks now
don't raise the oars from their pivots
fix your sharpest eye on the star
remain constant
don't blink but from time to time
sleep tranquilly on your fists
don't be afraid to remember
close your glass-cutting teeth
cage your tongue
don't swallow anymore

you have lost your reason, friend, now it's time
cut the cord
climb up to the wind
harden your heart

Translated by Patricia Santoro.

Ballerina

you dance anger chanting
and anger long and red like your heart
anger heart banner unfurled by the wound
in which you wrap yourself dancing
when you were born they swaddled your belly
they wrapped you while you were still wet
they put you in the cradle
your mother held you in her arms and suckled you
milk of tamarind and broom
your limbs grew long as branches
you braided your hair on windy nights
you wrapped yourself in anger dancing
and the dance was splendid
you danced the cold air
around the stars
you danced the rims of the bells
that opened when you were a child onto the surface of the sun

then someone said: nice girls don't dance

they clamped glasses over your eyes and heels on your feet
they hung purses on your arms and gloves on your hands
they sat you on red cushions so you could see better
they served you a banquet on silverservice
and they served you your own heart for lunch
you stayed at the table for quite a while
the whirlwind of your feet under the table

the whirlwind of your hands on the lace tablecloth
resting
chewing your heart
turning it with your tongue trying to swallow
others went dancing while you ate lunch
at five the milkman danced
at six the garbage man with gloves
at noon your sister went out
dancing her slipper daggers
at six they brought her home in an ambulance
they opened the door and her head rolled out
you got up screaming I can't
vomiting purses heels jewels gloves
dragging your anger through the streets
screaming though I ache and the child cries I dance
through the gyrating cranes and the rooftop ventilators
through the twisted bars and the rusted slabs of my dream armor
I dance
marking the edges of madness with red dots
my feet bleeding inside
I dance shoemakers and ice vendors on strike
I dance yellow trucks that make the earth tremble
I dance the no parking sign
no left turn
no u turn
stop
weeping weary sidewalks past the water in the gutters
twirling tristana on one leg
making whips with a truncated leg through the corridors
with your coral screens and your painted lips
with your bobbing breasts though the child cries Isadora I can't
stop dancing
though no one cares when I come and go
though Kafka tells me life wants nothing from you

---

it gets you when you're coming and leaves you when you go
then someone opens the window and throws her arms out
and you go in
twirling your slipper daggers through the banquet
slicing jaws and glass stems
twisting your anger banner red madwoman's face
through hollow eyes
you dance your heart on the table

Translated by Nancy Diáz.

To Be Seventeen Again

Violeta Parra

Violeta Parra (1904-1967), a Chilean folklorist and poet, is without a doubt one of the most resonant Latin American figures and one of the most important figures in Chilean popular culture. Violeta also distinguished herself as a popular singer and author of lyric works, among them *Al Son Los Dolores y Décimas – Autobiografía en Verso* (1967). With the passing of time, Violeta Parra is being recognized for her creativity in the field of lyric.

. . . .

I Curse in the Highest Sky
(Sirilla – song)

I curse in the highest sky
the star with its reflection,
I curse the bluish
flashes of the brook,
I curse the stone with shape
in the low ground,
I curse the fire of the furnace
because my soul is mourning,
I curse the statues of the time
with their embarassments,
how much more will my pain be.

I curse the mountains
of the Andes and the Coastal ranges,
I curse, dear Lord, the long
narrow belt of land,
likewise the peace and the war,
the frank and the fickle,
I curse the perfumed ones
because my longing is dead,
I curse all that is certain
and the false with the doubtful,
how much more will my pain be.

I curse the spring
with its gardens in flower
and the color of autumn
I truly curse;

the passing cloud
I curse it more and more
because grief is present.
I curse the entire winter
with the lying summer,
I curse the profane and the holy,
how much more will my pain be.

I curse the solitary
figure of the flag,
I curse any emblem
Venus and the Araucaria
the trill of the canary,
the cosmos and its planets,
the land and all its faults
because I am afflicted with sorrow,
I curse the wide sea
its ports and its fishing boats,
how much more will my pain be.

I curse moon and landscape,
the valleys and the deserts,
I curse dead for dead
and the living from king to servant,
the fowl with its plumage
I curse with stubbornness,
the classrooms, the sacristies
because a sorrow is hurting me,
I curse the word love
with all its filth,
how much more will my pain be.

I curse at last the white,
the black with the yellow,
bishops and altar boys,
ministers and preachers
I curse them crying;
the free and the imprisoned,
the soft and the quarrelsome,
I put my curse
in Greek and in Spanish
for the blame of a traitor,
how much more will my pain be.

Attention Young Bachelors
(Short popular song)

Attention young bachelors,
this I will explain to you:
just because you have money
don't say "I want to get married."

Don't say "I will have fun"
with my real wife,
the chains that will tie you down
are very strong.

It's most true that you will enjoy
those first months
but after the desire subsides
even your names will change.
Your names will be bread,
your names will be little onions.

And you will name yourself small pan
and will have the name of salt,
he who seeks the fertile rib
must think of all of this.

To men, they give the name potato
name them firewood and charcoal
name them box of dust
and also bar of soap,
will name them spoon,
knife and fork.
They name men plates and cups,
and they name them ladle —
when this happens it will be said:
"love is so very expensive."

And one piece is missing
that will soon be seen
as men come to know
the origin of their wives:
if she is jealous

if she imagines another woman.

There will not be joy or pleasure
money serves nothing
for this, young bachelors
you must pay close attention.

Why Is It This Way, Almighty God?

Why is it this way, Almighty God,
that the soul does not resign
when our calm is changed
by waves of sadness?
Perhaps it is the pride
of the one who receives the insult,
because the grief of seeing
the bud destroyed is too much.
Because they do not listen to the cooing,
indifference shoots forth.
Someone cries fiery tears
over the absence of a loved one,
the stirred heart
palpitates swiftly
at suddenly seeing itself
alone with great restlessness,
like a small sailboat
that's lost its captain
in the arms of a hurricane,
why is it this way, Almighty God?

Everyone talks of the summer,
of the spring,

of the moon, of the star
and of the reddened sky,
as if the one in love
ponders as much blue
as they have had, the virtue
that is eternally spoken of,
when only suddenly
the sound of the lute is heard.

The sadness is an inferno
that oppresses us as it pleases,
like a gluttonous bird
bites the brilliant flowers.
The soul is the governor
that rules the seasons,
reciprocated in love
being converted to sun
and in black the beautiful red clouds
if the man is in pain.

To Be Seventeen Again
(Sirilla – song)

To be seventeen again
after enduring a century
is to decipher symbols
without wisdom or competence,
to suddenly be again
most fragile like a second,
return to profound feeling
like a child in front of God,
that is how I feel

in this fertile moment.

My steps recede
when yours come forward,
the alliance of the arc
has pierced my nest,
has traveled through my veins
with all its colors
and even the hardened chain
that destiny has bound us to
is like a fine diamond
that lights my cloudless soul.

Reason has been unable to do
that which feeling can,
not the most clear action
nor the thought of most breadth,
everything is changed by the moment
like a condescending wizard,
that moves us sweetly away
from hatred and violence,
only love with its science
can return us to innocence.

Love is the whirlwind
of original purity,
even the wild animal
whispers its sweet trill,
detains the wanderers,
liberates the prisoners,
love with its concern
turns the aged into the young
and only love turns the evil one
into the pure and sincere.

The window wide open
it was opened like enchantment,
love came in with its shawl
like a tepid morning,
to the sound of beautiful "Diana,"
the jasmine burst forth,
love flying like a celestial being

hung earrings on the sky
the cherub converted
my years into seventeen

> *Refrain*

Love goes entangled, entangled,
like ivy to a wall,
and it shoots forth, shoots forth,
like small moss on the rock.
Ay, yes yes yes
ay, yes yes yes.

Translated by Shaun T. Griffin and Emma Sepúlveda-Pulvirenti.

Song For A Seed

So the years go by
and things are very different.
What was wine, today is dye,
what was leather, today is cotton
What was certain, today deception.
All I see is scarcity and loss,
today's laws shock me.
Spending my time confused
with great inertia
I seek relief in my song.

Time keeps flying
and things keep changing:
melosa grew in the wheat,

the sowing-back-breaking
the harvest-dwindling.
Truncated hope,
people never know
what awaits them tomorrow;
what awaits them tomorrow,
people never know.

I entered love's carnation
blinded by its colors,
captured by the brilliance
of such favored flower;
flattered by my passion
it left a bleeding sore,
beside myself, I weep
in this orchard of neglect.
Unresponsive carnation.
What wasted tears.

Life makes me fearful.
Its indifference terrifies me,
the hand of harshness
bound this blind knot . . .
my strength's been consumed
and my soul tormented
for me, what's called calm
is words with no meaning.

For a moment I walk
these streets with no direction
I see I'm in this world
with just the soul in my body.

Niggling treacheries
knot up my thoughts
Between the waters and wind
I'm lost in the distance.

I don't cry just to cry
but to quiet my mind
my tears like a prayer
fall on deaf ears.

I Thank Life for So Many Gifts

I thank life for so many gifts,
for my mind's windows, which I open
to see clearly, black and white,
the starred depths of the sky
and the man I love, lost in the crowd.

I thank life for so many gifts,
for my hearing that night and day
and all around records crickets,
canaries, hammers, turbines, barking,
squalls and my sweetheart's tender voice.

I thank life for so many gifts,
for sounds, the alphabet, and
the words I think and speak –
mother, friend, brother, and light
shining on the path of my lover's soul.

I thank life for so many gifts,
for the tread of my tired feet
wandering through cities and puddles,
beaches and deserts, mountains and plains,
your house, your street, and your garden.

I thank life for so many gifts,
for my heart which shakes its frame
as I see the fruits of the human brain,
as I face good so far from evil,
as I look into your deep clear eyes.

I thank life for so many gifts,
for laughter and tears, telling me
what is luck and what misfortune,
the two elements of my song
and your song – the same song,
and everyone's song – my own.

I thank life for so many gifts.

Translated by Bonnie Shepard.

At the Center of Injustice

Chile is bordered on the north by Peru
and by Cape Horn in the south.
Rising in the east is the mountain range
and in the west, the coastline glistens,
        the coastline glistens.

In the heartland lie the valleys with all their verdure
where the inhabitants proliferate.
Every family has many children;
miserably they live in the poorest of dwellings,
        the poorest of dwellings.

Of course, some people live in comfortable abundance,
but with the blood of the slaughtered staining their hands.
In full view of the arrogant coat of arms
argiculture poses its own probing questions,
        its own probing questions.

Several nations sell us the potato
although it is native to the south of Chile.
In full view of her tri-colored insignia,
mining, too, poses many difficulties,
        many difficulties.
The miner produces considerable cash,
but it goes right into the pockets of foreigners,
plentiful industry where for just a few pennies
there are laboring a great many women,
        a great many women.

And they are compelled to do so,
because what their husbands are paid
does not amount to enough to survive.
To steel myself against the sting of this hardship,
in the starry night I want to speak out,
        I want to speak out.

The homeland is beautiful, Mr. Tourist,
but they didn't show you the little shantytowns.
While you go on spending millions in a moment,

people are dying of hunger, which is everywhere,
    which is everywhere.

A great deal of money is in municipal parks,
while misery is widespread in the hospitals.
Right in the midst of the Avenue of Delights,
Chile is filled to its very core by injustice.

Because the Poor Have Nothing

Because the poor have
nowhere else to turn,
they turn to the heavens
with infinite hope
of finding what their brother
has left them in this world, little dove.
What things life holds, *zambitay!*

Because the poor have
nowhere to turn their voices,
they turn to the heavens
looking for an answer
since their brother does not hear
the voices of their hearts, little dove.
What things life holds, *zambitay!*

Because the poor have
no hope in this world,
they seek shelter in the other world
as a just balance.
For this reason, the processions,
the candles, and songs of praise, little dove.
What things life holds, *zambitay!*

From time immemorial
Hell was invented

to frighten the poor
with its eternal punishments.
And the poor, who are innocent,
in their innocence believe, little dove.
What things life holds, *zambitay!*

Heaven holds the reins,
the earth, and the money,
and the soldiers of the Pope
are well provided for,
and to those who work, they dole out
glory like a muzzle, little dove.
What things life holds, *zambitay!*
To perpetuate the lie
their confessor calls to them;
he tells them God does not want
any revolution at all,
nor demands, nor unions
that offend his heart, little dove.
What things life holds, *zambitay!*

Translated by Karen Kerschen.

Pita Amor

Pita Amor (1920) is one of Mexico's most inspirational and innovative artists. For many years she was the owner of a gallery where many artists, including Frida Kahlo, exhibited their works. Pita Amor is one of the few poets who continue to write in verse. Among her most well-known works are *Antología Poética* (1970) and *El Zoológico de Pita Amor* (1982).

. . . .

CXLII

The moon in her new era
the moon changing in the wind
and its eternal yen
has invited a chimera
to visit her. Hour
it was of the lunar orb,
the moon some star accord
to split her solitude,
the chimera is true
a Chinese bolt, thundered.

CXXXIX

Through Persia raving
the Phoenix gloomy
dwells in a gallery
of diamond trappings.
The Phoenix burning
I am in my eternal anxiety,
I am in my eternal reality,
in my loving blood
in my livid blood,
in my blood without piety!

CXXX

Like a mountain bristled
as an old pincushion
his body is not bright fuchsia
nor bloodied. Nor violated,
the dirty porcupine revered,
Christ of the animals
studded with crystals,
strolls his shadow on the wall
and his mature calm
is an accomplice of his evils.

CXXXIV

The sea serpent is
the owner of the salt waters,
of the skies and altars
that take her tongue, delicate.
The divine serpent is
of three heads, the goddess,
butterfly, one of those
that fly from sea to the sky,
the serpent is my desire.
The hydra broken in pieces!

Translated by Shaun T. Griffin and Emma Sepúlveda-Pulvirenti.

AFTERWORD

The multiplicty of voices included in this anthology testifies to the diversity of styles and texts existing within the collective space of women's poetic discourse in the Americas.

Reflected in the organizational divisions which frame this volume are metaphors and desires which allude to its rebellious, introspective, creative, and sometimes haunting language. It soon becomes apparent that women who have written and continue to write poetry in the Americas are not restricted by subject matter nor by the linguistic conventions that have stereotypically defined them through the centuries. These are women who write with a deep sense of personal conviction and often courage. They are powerful innovators of language as well as visionaries of a broad cultural perspective that exceeds identification with issues of gender, race, or ethnicity.

These Are Not Sweet Girls is appropriately named for as their poems reveal, the women whose work comprises this volume dare to subvert traditional boundaries and assert themselves intrepidly before the canonical legacy of their male counterparts. Some of the images that they create strike us with their audacity, while they at the same time reveal that women have on occasion rejected the traditional submissive posture associated with their sex for one that is more assertive, responsive, and human.

As bold and daring as many of them are, however, it would be erroneous to classify them all as feminists in the traditional sense of the term. Some of the voices are more politically committed than others. Be that as it may, they are all acutely aware of their condition as women and of the necessity to record their own histories so that their common legacy as women writers be identified with a culture that had for centuries excluded them from the literary mainstream.

Several generations of poets are included in this anthology and more than a dozen Central and South American countries are represented through the selections that have been made. What makes this particular collection unique is that as diverse as the voices and styles are, by gathering them together in a multi-colored tapestry of textures and images, Marjorie Agosín challenges the conventional ordering of anthologized texts and insightfully encourages us as readers to search for the common threads that unite them.

As the volume itself reveals, women have always felt strongly connected with words and with their intricate relationships and meanings, words which for Alejandra Pizarnick are like "lonely, desolate women" singing out through a voice that she hears in the distance.

The words that these women recite and sing through their lyrical discourses are the gateways through which we as readers come to know them and to comprehend their personal and public histories. They are the means through which we may also participate in an ever-expanding cultural landscape that is not limited by geographical boundaries.

Since this is not a bilingual edition, we must depend solely upon the judgments of the individual translators who have tried to render as faithfully as possible the essence and flavor of the original texts. A good translator will always question the choices that he or she makes and will avoid images and/or associations that deviate, however subtly, from the source, thereby changing its inherent meaning. Sometimes creative liberties must be taken, but only when a new mode of expression is found that can be more effectively convey the full experience of the original without jeopardizing its integrity.

Rolando Costa Picazo, the well-known Argentine translator, believes that the different languages that we speak condition our thoughts and our vision of life. He also percieves translation as an art form capable of crossing national barriers. In his own words, it is "a vehicle or a bridge, through which cultures travel."[1]

Translation as a process transcends the literal and exists in a realm that fluctuates between the intuitive and creative capacities of the individual whose primary goal is to maintain as closely as possible fidelity to the original text. The final product should appear as if it were executed with the spontaneity of the original.

Translation is above all an act of recreation. It is the responsibility of the translator to transmit another's vision of life into another culture by passing it through the filtering system of one's own unique vision without corrupting it in the process. Recreation in this case does not imply an overhauling and restoration of the original but rather a reconstruction or revival of the source language into another tongue, in this case English, that will communicate a shared vision that is charged with the same emotional impact and intent of the original. The hoped-for effect is one that will establish another vital link between two different yet mutualy accessible communities. The most powerful challenge confronting the translator is to search for the best and most effective means to bring together these culturally-inspired visions that will connect with one another and enrich the artistic landscapes of their reading public.

Such was the challenge confronting the translators of this anthology who through their word choices attempted to capture the creative intensity and substance of the Spanish originals. Their interpretations of the poems create the apertures through which we as readers may begin our journey into the vast cultural mosaic of twentieth century women's poetry in the Americas.

The women poets collected together in this volume challenge their exclusion or "limited access" to the culture-making processes and contribute through their discourse to the task of renaming and restructuring the world by enriching it with their distinctive voices. They write about a diverse array of subjects ranging from love, erotic desire, friendship, motherhood, family, politics, aesthetics, and work to oppression, alienation, metaphysical anguish, freedom, and hope. As different as their voices appear on the surface, one senses that the women whose poems compose this inspiring collection are held together by the experiences of a shared sisterhood that struggles to reclaim and to re-define its space in a world where gender will no longer be an instrument of power, rupture, and oppression.

These are women who by repossessing the Logos and by creating their own innovative zones of discourse not only dismantle old stereotypes but also invite us to participate in a reality that can no longer be dismissed as peripheral and minor. As Marjorie Agosín so poignantly observes in her introduction, these women are narrators of their own destiny and create images that defy us with their every word. Through their distinct yet similar voices, we are reminded that there are other ways of seeing, feeling, and telling that are an integral part of the broader culture in all its pluralistic dimensions. *These Are Not Sweet Girls* is a volume that transcends itself and corroborates the conviction that among other things, as Tillie Olsen has stated, "conscience and world sensibility are as natural to women as to men; men have been free to develop and exercise them, that is all."[2]

> — Celeste Kostopulos-Cooperman
> Suffolk University
> Boston, MA

1 - Paula Burbin, "The Art of Rolando Costa Picazo," unpublished essay.
2 - Tillie Olson, Silences (New York: Delta/Seymour Lawrence, 1965.) p. 42.

THE TRANSLATORS

Chris Allen is a poet and translator who lives in New York City. He has done a bilingual translation of Carlota Caulfield's collection *Sometimes I Call Myself Childhood.*

Zoe Anglesey's book *Something More Than Force: Poems for Guatemala, 1971-1982* received honorable mentin from the Before Columbus Foundation's American Book Awards in 1983. Her translations appear in *Costa Rica: A Literary Travel Companion* and in *Mouth to Mouth: Poems by Twelve Contemporary Mexican Women.* She has edited three anthologies: *Stone on Stone, Word Up! Hope for Youth Poetry,* and *Ixok Amar Go: Central American Women's Poetry for Peace.* She teaches writing at Baruch College and Long Island University in New York and is a senior editor at the *Voice Literary Supplement.*

Susan Bassnett is one of the most distinguished theorists of Latin American literature, as well as a poet and novelist. She is a professor of comparative literature at the University of Warwick in England.

Sally Cheney Bell was born in Boston, Massachusetts in 1928 and graduated from Radcliffe College in 1949 with a B.A. in Language and Literature. She served as a free-lance translator, primarily for the United States Government, during the years 1979-1988. She has been an active member of the American Translators Association since 1979 and currently resides in Keene, New Hampshire.

Magda Bogin is a writer, translator, and journalist. She has been a National Fellow and has been awarded two grants from the National Endowment for the Arts. She has published many translations, among them *House of the Spirits* by Isabel Allende.

Pamela Carmell is a translator of Central American poets. She lives in San Francisco.

Daisy Cocco De Filippis is a professor of Latin American literature and Associate Dean at York College. She has edited numerous anthologies on Dominican women poets.

Diana P. Decker teaches Spanish at George Mason University in Virginia. Her translation of Cristina Peri Rossi's book of poems *Babel*

Barbara won the *Quartrly Review of Literature*'s 1992 international poetry competition. Her translation of Peri Rossi's *Evohé - Poemas Eróticos* was published by Azul Editions in 1994.

Nancy Diáz is a professor of Caribbean studies at Rutgers University.

Patricia Dubrava specializes in the review of Latin American literature for the *Bloomsbury Review* and has published numerous essays and poems. Her book of poems, *Choosing the Moon,* was published in 1981, and her poems have since appeared in six anthologies. Some of her translations of the poetry of Elsa Cross appreared in *The Guadalupe Review* in 1991. She lives in Denver, Colorado.

Darwin Flakoll has worked extensively as a correspondent for a number of western newspapers and for the International Feature Service. Over the years, he has collaborated with his wife, Claribel Alegría, on books of testimony, Latin American history, and literary anthologies. His recent translation of Alegría's book *Fugues* was published by Curbstone Press in 1993.

Cola Franzen is a respected literary translator and writer who currently makes her home in Cambridge, MA. She has collaborated with Marjorie Agosín on numerous occasions, most recently as translator of *Sargasso* (White Pine Press, 1994). Her translations and articles frequently appear in literary magazines and journals.

Monica Bruno Galmozzi is a graduate of Wellesley College and received her M.A. in Spanish Literature from Columbia University in New York. She has collaborated with Marjorie Agosín on numerous projects. One of her translations appeared in *Secret Weavers: Stories of the Fantastic by Women of Argentina and Chile.*

Janet N. Gold is a professor of Latin American literature at Louisiana State University in Baton Rouge. She is the author of *Clementina Suárez: Her Life and Poetry,* forthcoming from the University of Florida Press. She has published numerous articles on Latin American women writers.

Shaun T. Griffin is a poet and translator. He, along with collaborator Emma Sepúlveda-Pulvirenti, received the Carolyn Kizer Foreign Language and Translation Prize from Calpaooya College in 1992. He edited *Desert Wood: An Anthology of Nevada Poets* and *Torn by Light,* both of which were published by the University of Nevada Press. *Snowmelt,* a volume of his own poetry, was released from Black Rock Press in 1994. He directs Nevada's homeless youth education office and runs a prison poetry workshop which produces the annual journal *Razor Wire.*

Karen Kerschen graduated from The Cooper Union for the Advancement of Science and Art with a degree in fine art. She has worked as a photojournalist, has co-produced a television documentary about the situation in Chile, and co-curated two exhibits of contemporary Chilean *arpilleras.* She sang Latin American music for seven years with La Pena Cultural Center's chorus. She lives and works in Sunnyvale, CA.

Kathryn A. Kopple currently resides in Philadelphia, Pennsylvania. She is a specialist in contemporary Latin American poetry and has translated works by Mercedes Roffé, Marosa Di Giorgio and Ana Clavel. Selections from Roffé's *Subchamber* in English have been published in literary reviews in both the United States and Canada.

Celeste Kostopulos-Cooperman is a professor of Humanities and Modern Languages at Suffolk University, Boston, MA. Her book, *The Lyrical Vision of María Luisa Bombal,* was published by Tamesis Press, London, in 1988, and her translations of Latin American women writers and poets have appeared extensively. She won the ALTA Prize in 1993 for her translation of Marjorie Agosín's *Circles of Madness* (White Pine Press, 1992).

Maria Jacketti was born in 1960 in Hazelton, Pennsylvania. In addition to being a translator, she is also a fiction writer, poet, and college instructor. She has translated Pablo Neruda's *Las piedras del cielo, Garden Odes, Cantos Ceremoniales* and co-translated *Maremoto: Seaquake* (White Pine Press, 1993) with Dennis Maloney.

Suzanne Jill Levine is a prolific translator of Latin American writing, including works by Manuel Puig, Carlos Fuentes, Adolfo Bioy Casares, José Donoso, and others. Her own book, *The Subversive Scribe: Translating Latin American Fiction,* was published in 1992 by Graywolf Press.

Mark McCaffrey is a professor of Spanish at the University of Vermont. His translations of poetry and fiction have been published in numerous literary journals. Recipient of a National Endowment for the Humanities Fellowship, he spent the sumer of 1994 at the University of Chicago.

Arthur Natella is a professor of Latin American literature at the University of New Mexico at Las Cruces and author of numerous essays and books about Latin American literature.

Tess O'Dwyer has a Masters in English from Rutgers University. Her translation of *Empire of Dreams* won the 1991 Columbia University Translation Center Award. Her translations have appeared in numerous journals including *The Prose Poem, AGNI, The Literary Review, Sonora Review* and *The Dickinson Review.*

Dave Oliphant, a prolific poet (*Austin, Maria's Poems, On a High Horse,* and other titles) has won the Austin Book Award. He is an editor at the University of Texas-Austin Humanities Research Center. He has edited and translated anthologies of Peruvian, Chilean, and Mexican poetry. He is best known for his translation of Chilean poet Enrique Lihn.

Louise B. Popkin is a professional translator and lecturer in Spanish (Harvard University) and translation (University of Massachusetts). Her translations of Latin American prose, poetry, and drama have appeared in a number of anthologies and literary journals. Most recently, she translated and edited, with Sául Sosnowski, the volume *Repression, Exile, and Democracy: Uruguayan Culture* (Duke University Press, 1993.)

Joy Renjilian Burgy has, for fifteen years, been a faculty member at a Wellesley College where she has taught all levels of Spanish language as well as Caribbean literature and culture and Hispanic literature of the United States. She currently serves as director of the Mellon Minority Undergraduate Fellowship Program and is a visiting lecturer at Harvard University Extension School. Co-editor of *Album: Cuentos del mundo hispánico,* her translations of selected works of Rosario Ferré, Elena Poniatowska, Amalia Rendic, and Nancy Morejón have appeared in various literary anthologies.

Alison Ridley is a professor of Latin American literature at Hollins College and author of essays on Golden Age literature.

Emma Jane Robinett has taught English and English as a second language at York College, CUNY, and Polytechnic University of New York. A poet and translator, she has been lauded by the Academy of American Poets.

Patricia Santoro, a native of New Jersey, received her Ph.D. from Rutgers University. *Novel into Film: The Case of La familia de Pascual Duarte and Los santos inocentes* was published in 1995.

Emma Sepúlveda-Pulvirenti, a native of Chile, is professor of Latin American literature at the University of Nevada, Reno. She is also a poet and photographer and author of numerous boks of literary criticism and poetry.

Bonnie Shepard is a public health worker and director of health programs for the Ford Foundation in Santiago, Chile.

Heather Rosario Sievert has published her translations and reviews in numerous magazines and journals. Her work has also appeared in several anthologies, and a large collection of her translations of Cuban poet Nancy Morejon's work is forthcoming.

Mary Jane Treacy is professor of Spanish and Women's Studies at Simmons College. Her translations of short stories by Cristina Peri Rossi have appeared in *Secret Weavers: Stories of the Fantastic* and in *A Forbidden Passion.*

Paula Vega is a native of the Dominican Republic and a graduate of Wellesley College. She has worked with Marjorie Agosin in translating and trnascribing many of her works and has worked independently on projects of creative writing, human rights, and democracy.

Ellen Watson has translated eight Brazilian novels, including *The Tree of the Seventh Heaven.* She is the translation editor of *The Massachusetts Review.* She received a National Endowment for the Arts Translation Fellowship, which enabled her to finish the translations in *The Alphabet in the Park: Selected Poems of Adélia Prado.*

Oliver Welden, a native of Santiago, Chile, is the author of *Anhista* and *Perro del Amor,* which won the National Poetry Award from the Society of Chilean Writers. He was co-editor of the poetry journal *Tebaida* (Chile: 1968-73). He has translated poetry for *Studia Hispánica, The Journal of the University of Chile, The International Poetry Review,* among others. He is professor of English at the University of Tennessee.

Alan West was born in Havana, Cuba and raised in Puerto Rico. A writer, poet, and translator, he has taught at Wellesley Colege, New York University, Boston University, Fordham College, and Babson College. His published work includes *En cinco tiempos, Dándole nombres a la lluvia,* and *Jose Marti.* His most recent work is a biography of baseball player Roberto Clemente.

Steven F. White is the editor and translator of the bilingual anthologies *Poets of Chile: 1965-1985, Poets of Nicaragua: 1916-1979,* and *From Eve's Rib: Selected Poems of Gioconda Belli* as well as the author of a book of critical essays, *Modern Nicaraguan Poetry: Dialogues with France and the United States.* His most recent book of poems is *From the Country of Thunder.* He currently teaches at St. Lawrence University in Canton, New York.

Carolyne Wright, a poet, translator and literary critic, received M.A. and D.A. degrees from Syracuse University. She has been a Fulbright Scholar and has won numerous awards including the 1990 PEN/ Jerard Fund Award, the Academy of American Poets Prize, a Witter Bynner Foundation Grant, and the Pablo Neruda Prize. The author of ten books, her most recent collection is *In Order to Speak With the Dead,* translations of the poems of Jorge Tellier. She presently lives in Arlington, MA.

Acknowledgements (Continued)

"The Blood of Others," "Birth," "Nicaragua Water Fire," and "Brief Lessons in Eroticism" from *From Eve's Rib* by Gioconda Belli. Translated by Steven F. White. (Curbstone Press, 1989). Copyright 1989 by Gioconda Belli. Translation copyright 1989 by Steven F. White. Used with the permission of Curbstone Press.

"Accounting," "Ars Poetica," "Erosion," "Nocturnal Visits," "Silence," "The Grandmother," "Have Pity" from *Fugues* by Claribel Alegría. Translated by D. J. Flakoll (Curbstone Press, 1993). Copyright 1993 by Claribel Alegría. Translation copyright 1993 by D. J. Flakoll. Used with the permission of Curbstone Press.

"Glance," "Greek Metamorphosis," "And Here are the Poets In their Sad Portraits," "Women Don't Die on the Front Lines," "Poet's Biography," "For the Moment," and "Creed" copyright 1989 by Belkis Cuza Malé. Translations copyright 1989 by Pamela Carmell. Reprinted by permission of Alan Brilliant, Unicorn Press.

"Opprobium" and "Message" copyright 1994 Rosario Ferré. Translation copyright 1994 Rosario Ferré. "You Have Lost, They Tell Me, Your Reason" copyright 1980 by Rosario Ferré. Translation copyright 1980 by Patricia Santoro. "Ballerina" copyright 1980 by Rosario Ferré. Translation copyright 1980 by Nancy Gray Díaz Reprinted by permission of the translators and of Susan Bergholz Literary Services, New York.

"In the Life and Death of Rosamel del Valle" and "Creation" copyright 1980 by Eunice Odio. Translations copyright 1980 by Arthur Natella. Reprinted from *The Renewal of the Vision: Voices of Latin American Women Poets 1940-1980,* Marjorie Agosín and Cola Franzen, editors, by permission of Paul Green, Spectacular Diseases.

Poems from "Palabrarmás" copyright 1992 by Ceculia Vicuña. Translations copyright 1992 by Eliot Weinberger and Suzanne Jill Levine. Reprinted from *Unravelling Words & the Weaving of Water* with the permission of Graywolf Press, Saint Paul, Minnesota.

Poems by Cristina Peri Rossi copyright 1971 Cristina Peri Rossi. Translation copyright 1994 by Diana P. Decker. Reprinted from *Evohé* (1994) with the permission of Azul Editions.

All poems by Gabriela Mistral are from *A Gabriela Mistral Reader,* White Pine Press, 1993. Translations copyright 1993 by Maria Jacketti.

"When She Showed Me Her Photograph" and "Memorial" copyright 1992 by

An exhaustive effort has been made to locate all rights holders and to clear reprint permissions. This process has been complicated, and if any required acknowledgements have been overlooked it is unintentional and forgiveness is requested. If notified, the publishers will be pleased to rectify any omission in future editions.